EDUCATION IN INDIA

About the Author

J.C. Aggarwal (*b.* 1928), has a varied experience in the field of education. He was Deputy Director of Education and Executive Director of Education and Executive Director of Delhi Bureau of Text Books under Delhi Administration. He has organised and attended many conferences, seminars and workshops on education. Shri Aggarwal has authored more than hundred books on various aspects of social sciences.

Sarita Aggarwal (*b.* 1957) is presently working as a Post-Graduate Teacher in Modern School, Vasant Vihar, New Delhi. She takes a keen interest in current educational through, problems and practices.

EDUCATION IN INDIA

(A Comparative Study of States and Union Territories)

J.C. AGGARWAL
SARITA AGGARWAL

CONCEPT PUBLISHING COMPANY PVT. LTD.
NEW DELHI-110059

ISBN: 978-81-7022-286-6

Edition 2023

Published and Printed by

Concept
Since 1974

Concept Publishing Company Pvt. Ltd.
A/15-16, Commercial Block, Mohan Garden,
New Delhi-110059 (India)
T: 91-11-41101460
E: publishing@conceptpub.com, *W*: www.conceptpub.com

Preface

To Know Thyself, Compare Thyself with Others

An attempt has been made for the first time to make a comparative study of the development of various aspects of education in the States and the Union Territories of India, on the basis of total population and school going population wherever possible in the respective age group.

The book is divided into eight chapters. Chapter 1 provides an overview of Administration, Management, Planning and Financing of Education in India. Chapter 2 deals with the States having the best position and its reverse in respect to enrolment ratios, pupil-teacher ratio, percentage of trained teachers, enrolment per 10,000 inhabitants etc., besides listing States in all these areas in their ranking order. Similarly, Chapter 3 incorporates comparative data on all types of institutions from pre-primary to higher education. Chapter 4 gives comparative data on diverse issues like vocational facilities. Chapters 5 and 6 present educational profile of each State and Union Territory respectively covering 35 items. Chapter 7 illustrates an All India Profile in education in respect of 39 items. Chapter 8 denotes the development of education at a glance in India in its various facets during the period 1950-51 to 1986-87.

The data in this book have been primarily derived/obtained from "Selected Educational Statistics, 1986-87", Ministry of Human Resource Development (Department of Education), Government of India (1988). Other sources are : Annual Report, 1988-89, Ministry of Human Resource Development; Fifth All-India Educational Survey: Selected Statistics, NCERT (1989) and Development of Education, 1986-88: National Report of India, National Institute of Educational Planning and Administration (1988).

It is observed that there seems to be no uniform system of the maintenance of educational statistics in India with the result that at times it becomes very difficult to reconcile data collected even by National Agencies. For instance though the reference data i.e. 30 September, 1986 are the same in the statistics compiled by the Ministry and the

NCERT, yet the figures do not agree in several cases. It is, therefore, very urgent to devise an uniform nomenclature in this regard. All figures in the book relate to the latest year 1986-87 except where otherwise stated.

Statistics comprises the science of decision-making in education in the face of uncertainty. It would be too much to say that statistics in its present state of development, can handle all situations involving uncertainties. However, new methods are constantly developed and it can be said that modern statistics provides the framework for looking at situations in a logical way. Numerical data derived from surveys and other sources constitutes the new material on which interpretations, analysis and decisions are made and it is essential to know how to squeeze usable information from such data.

As observed in the Preface to 'Selected Educational Statistics: 1986-87 (1988)': "the information given in this publication has been collected from the States. These are not subjected to detailed scrutiny and as such may be regarded as provisional". Nevertheless the data provide general trends and direction for future action.

We are confident that this publication will serve to fill up the need for a handy and reliable reference manual and prove of immense use to a large number of readers – educators, educational administrators, managers and planners, research workers and writers.

A few limitations and gaps are inevitable in a collection of this type, for which the compilers crave the indulgence of the readers.

J.C. AGGARWAL
SARITA AGGARWAL

Contents

Preface 5
List of Figures 11

1. **Overview : Administration, Management, Planning and Financing of Education in India** 13

Role of the Central and State Governments
Educational Administration at the Central Level
Educational Administration at the State Level
Educational Planning at the Central and State Levels
Administration, Planning and Financing of Education in the National Policy on Education

2. **Comparative Educational Data on States : Enrolment Ratios and Vocational Facilities** 21

States with the Best Positions in Different Areas of Education
States with the Most Unfavourable Positions in Different Areas of Education
States with the Highest and the Lowest Enrolment Ratio in Classes I to VIII
States with Maximum and Minimum Vocational Facilities

3. **Comparative Educational Data on States : Institutions** 35

States with the Most Favourable situation regarding Number of Institutions per 10 Lakhs of Inhabitants
States with the most Favourable Situation in Respect of Number of Inhabitants per Institution
States with the Most Unfavourable Situation in Respect of Number of Inhabitants per Institution

Percentage of Rural Population with Primary Schools/ Sections within the Habitation

Figs 3. 1 to 3.7 showing Number of Different Types of Institutions – Primary Schools, Middle Schools, High/Post Basic Schools, Higher Secondary Schools, Junior/Intermediate Colleges, Arts/Science/ Commerce Collegesand Universities in the Ranking Order Serving per 10 lakhs of inhabitants (population).

Fig. 3.8 showing Number of Teacher Training Colleges per 50 Lakhs of Inhabitants

Figs. 3.9 and 3.10 showing Number of Institutions including Preprimary and Primary, respectively, Per 10 Lakhs of Inhabitants.

4. **Comparative Study of Diverse Issues in Education in States** 49

Table 4.1 : Number of Institutions offering Vocational Courses at +2 Stage and Enrolment

Table 4.2 : States with the Best (Lowest) and Unfavourable (Maximum) Pupil-Teacher Ratio

Table 4.3 : Pupil-Teacher Ratio at Various Stages in States 53

Table 4.4 : Percentage of Trained Teachers at Various levels in States

Table 4.5 : Secondary Teacher Training Institutions: Statewise and Universitywise

Table 4.6 : Per Capita Budgeted Expenditure on Education – Statewise with Ranking

Table 4.7 : Percentage at Budgeted Expenditure on Education to Total Budget (Revenue Account) -- Statewise with Ranking

Table 4.8 : Number and Percentage of One Teacher School : Statewise

Table 4.9 : Literacy Rates of States and Union Territories

5. **State Education Profile** 65

Table 5.1 to 5.22 covering 16 Types of Institutions from Pre-primary to University and 19 categories of Enrolment from Pre-Primary to Ph.D.

6. **Union Territory Education Profile** 89

Tables 6.1 to 6.11 covering 16 Types of Institutions from Pre-primary to University and 19 categories of Enrolement from Pre-Primary to Ph.D. 113-130
Fig. 6.1 Enrolment at H'gher Secondary/Pre-University/ Intermediate Level
Fig. 6.2 : Enrolment in B.E./B.Sc. Engg. Per 10,000 Population
Fig. 6.2(a) : Enrolment in B.A./B.Sc./B.Com. Per 10,000 Population

7. **All India Education Profile** 103

Table 7.1 : Enrolment (by Classes) in India
Table 7.2 : Category and Number of Institutions in India
Fig. 7.1 : Population in India : 1951 to 1988
Fig. 7.2 : Literacy Rate : 1950-51, 1981 and 1985
Fig. 7.3 : Elementary Education : 1950-51 to 1986-87
Fig. 7.4 : Women Higher Education

8. **Development of Education in India : Plan Period 1950-51 to 1986-87** 111

Table 8.1 : Sector-wise Plan/Non-Plan Revised Estimates for Education Departments of States/Union Territories and Centre (Revenue Account) for 1986-87
Table 8.2 and Fig. 8.1 : Growth of Educational Institutions
Table 8.3 and Fig. 8.2 : Number of Students by Education Stage
Table 8.4 and Fig. 8.3 : Girls Enrolment by Stages
Table 8.5 and Fig. 8.4 : Number of Teachers
Table 8.6 and Fig. 8.5 and 8.6 : Progress of Technical Education

Index 119

List of Figures

2.1 Enrolment Ratio in Classes I to V (General Education) 27
2.2 Enrolment Ratio in Classes VI to VIII (General Education) 28
2.3 Enrolment at High/Post Basic Stage/Classes per 10,000 Popultion (Inhabitants) 29
2.4 Enrolment at Higher Secondary (Old and New Pattern/. Pre University/Intermediate per 10,000 Inhabitants) 30
2.5 Enrolment in B.A./B.Sc./B.Com. Per 10,000 Population 31
2.6 Enrolment in M.A./M.Sc./M.Com. Per 10,000 Inhabitants 32
2.7 Enrolment Per 10,000 Inhabitants (All Stages) 33
3.1 Number of Primary/Junior Basic Schools Per 10 Lakhs of Population 39
3.2 Number of Middle/Senior Basic School Per 10 Lakhs of Population 40
3.3 Number of High/Post-Basic School Per 10 Lakhs of Population 41
3.4 Number of Higher Secondary 10+2 Schools Per 10 Lakhs of Population 42
3.5 Number of Junior/Intermediate Colleges Per 10 Lakhs of Population 43
3.6 Number of Arts/Science/Commerce Colleges Per 10 Lakhs of Population 44
3.7 Number of Universities Per 10 Lakhs of Population 45
3.8 Number of Teachers Training Colleges Per 50 Lakhs of Inhabitants 46
3.9 Number of Institutions Per 10 Lakhs of Inhabitants (Excluding Pre Primary) 47
3.10 Number of Institutions (Excluding Pre-Primary and Primary) Per 10 Lakhs of Inhabitants 48
6.1 Enrolment at Higher Secondary/Pre-University/ Intermediate Level 100
6.2 (a) Enrolment in B.E./B.Sc. Engg. Per 10,000 Population 101
6.2 (b) Enrolment in B.A./B.Sc./B.Com. Per 10,000 Population 102

7.1	Population in India, 1951 to 1988	106
7.2	Literacy Rate, 1950-51, 1981, 1985	107
7.3	Elementary Education, 1950-51 to 1986-87	108
7.4	Women Higher Education	109
8.1	Growth of Educational Institutions (Schools)	114
8.2	Growth of Enrolment	115
8.3	Percentage of Girls' Enrolment to Total Enrolment	116
8.4	Growth of Teachers	117
8.5	Technical Education (Number of Institutions)	118
8.6	Technical Education (Enrolment)	118

1

OVERVIEW:
Administration, Management, Planning and Financing of Education

Role of the Central and State Governments

India is an Union of States with a Parliamentary form of Government both at the Union and State levels. Till 1976, education, subject to a few provisions, was a State responsibility. The 42nd amendment to the Constitution effected in 1976 made education a concurrent subject thereby investing the Parliament with the authority to legislate on education. However no such legislation has yet been enacted by the Parliament. Efforts have been mainly to arrive at a meaningful partnership between the Union Government and the State Governments. Thus administration is a shared responsibility of the Centre and the State Governments.

Educational Administration at the Central Level

Administration of education at the national level is carried out through the Department of Education and its agencies which operate as part of the Ministry of Human Resource Development (MHRD). The Ministry of Human Resource Development is headed by a Cabinet Minister of the Union Government while a Minister of State is placed directly in charge of the Education portfolio. Within the MHRD the Department of Education consists of a number of divisions/units dealing with various aspects of educational development in policy-making. The Secretariat of the Department of Education is headed by a Secretary and is supported by Special Secretaries and Education Advisors at different levels in dealing with academic and policy matters of education. The Department of Education is directly responsible for the administration and financing of certain national and regional institutions which are created by the Central Government through an act of the Parliament or otherwise. In addition, Department of Education at the Centre is also responsible for providing direction and guidance to the authorities dealing with education in the various State Governments and Union Territory Administrations with regard to formulation and implementation of education plans and programmes. The Department of Education at the Centre also initiates and implements certain programmes related to education at various levels. Monitoring the progress of these programmes is also the responsibility of the Department of Education at the Centre. The Department of Education also brings out periodical publications containing statistical and other information related to educational programmes and progress achieved in respect of them.

Educational Administration at the State Levels

For all practical purposes the State governments have the complete responsibility for administration of school education; in some of the States, local self-government bodies such as Panchayat Samities, Municipal Corporation etc. have also been associated with a view to making the system of administration sensitive to the local conditions and also to facilitate the participation of local communities. In higher education, on the other hand, while State Governments continue to hold the major responsibility of administering and financing of higher education, they are, by and large, required to operate through universities and other autonomous institutions which essentially function according to the guidelines provided by the University Grants Commission. In other words, while school education is predominantly a local-State partnership, higher education operates as an area of Centre-State Partnership.

Educational Planning at the Central and State Level

Educational planning in the country is essentially the joint endeavour of the Central and State Governments. The Planning Commission at the Centre and the State Planning Departments decide the policy and approach to be adopted for the development of education in the country. A planning and monitoring division in the Central Ministry works in close liaison with the education division of the Planning Commission. On the basis of broad guidelines issued by the Planning Commission, draft five year plans and annual plans are prepared by the Central Ministries and the State Governments. These Plans are discussed and examined at various levels before being finally approved for implementation.

Actions related to education at the national level including planning and policy-making are guided and coordinated by the Central Advisory Board of Education, the members of which include Ministers of Education of different States and Union Territories and leading educationists of the country. Coordination of planning and implementation of educational programmes in the country is also facilitated through such forums as the State Education Ministers Conference, the Conference of Education Secretaries and the Planning Commission of the Government of India. For the planning and administration of education, each State Government has its own machinery and each

State/Union Territory is divided into a number of districts which are further divided into blocks/mandals. This district is the most important unit of educational administration in various States. The District Education Officer (DEO) in most States is generally overall in-charge of elementary as well as secondary education. The DEO is supported by a number of officers who directly deal with secondary education in the district. At each block level a Block Education Officer is in-charge of elementary and non-formal education programmes within the respective block. The Block Educational Officers function under the overall guidance and control of the District Education Officer for administrative purposes. The system, however, is not uniform in all the States and Union Territories.

The bulk of the expenditure i.e. about 65 per cent is borne by the States. The Finance Commission transfers resources at the end of each plan to each State under : (i) Share in Income-tax (ii) Share in Excise, and (iii) Lump sum Grant-in-Aid.

Budget provision for education in India as a whole has to be seen as the aggregate of the budget provisions made by the Central Government and various States and Union Territories. It has also to be seen in terms of provisions made under plan as well as non-plan sectors.

Departments, other than the Departments of Education in States/Union Territories and Ministries at the Centre, other than the Ministry of Human Resource Development also incur some expenditure on education.

Administration, Planning and Financing of Education in the National Policy on Education

An overhaul of the system of planning and the management of education will receive high priority. The guiding considerations will be:

(a) Evolving a long-term planning and management perspective of education and its integration with the country's developmental and manpower needs;
(b) Decentralisation and the creation of a spirit of autonomy for education of non-governmental agencies and voluntary effort;
(c) Giving pre-eminence to people's involvement including association of non-governmental agencies and voluntary effort;
(d) Inducing more women in the planning and management of education;

(e) Establishing the principle of accountability in relation to given objectives and norms.

National Level

The Central Advisory Board of Education (CABE) will play a pivotal role in reviewing educational development, determining the changes required to improve the system and monitoring implementation. It will function through appropriate committees and other mechanisms created to ensure contact with, and coordination among the various areas of Human Resource Development. The Department of Education at the Centre and in the States will be strengthened through the involvement of professionals.

Indian Education Service

A proper management structure in education will entail the establishment of the Indian Education Service as an All-India Service. It will bring a national perspective to this vital sector. The basic principles, functions and procedures of recruitment to this service will be decided in consultation with the State Governments.

State Level

State Governments may establish State Advisory Boards of Education on the lines of CABE. Effective measures should be taken to integrate mechanisms in the various State departments concerned with Human Resource Development.

Special attention will be paid to the training of educational planners, administrators and heads of insitutions. Institutional arrangements for this purpose should be set up in stages.

District and Local Levels

District Boards of Education will be created to manage education up to the higher secondary level. State governments will attend to this aspect with all possible expedition. Within a multi-level framework of educational development, Central, State, district and local level agencies will participate in planning, coordination, monitoring and evaluation.

A very important role must be assigned to the head of an educational institution. Heads will be specially selected and trained. School complexes will be promoted on a flexible pattern so as to serve as networks of institutions and synergic alliances to encourage professionalism among teachers, to ensure observance of norms of conduct and to enable the sharing of experiences and facilities. It is expected that a developed system of school complexes will take over much of the inspection functions in due course.

Local communities, through appropriate bodies, will be assigned a major role in programmes of school improvement.

Voluntary Agencies and Aided Institutions

Non-government and voluntary effort including social activist groups will be encouraged, subject to proper management, and financial assistance provided . At the same time, steps will be taken to prevent the establishment of institutions set up to commercialise education.

Resources

The Education Commission of 1964-66, the National Education Polic of 1968 and practically all others concerned with education hav stressed that the egalitarian goals and the practical, developmen oriented objectives of Indian society can be realised only by makir investments in education of an order commensurate with the nature ar dimensions of the task.

Resources, to the extent possible, will be raised by mobilisir donations, asking the beneficiary communities to maintain scho buildings and supplies of some consumables, raising fees at the highe levels of education and effecting some savings by the efficient use c facilities. Institutions involved with research and the development c technical and scientific manpower should also mobilize some funds b levying a cess or charge on the user agencies, including governme departments, and entrepreneurs. All these measures will be taken nc only to reduce the burden on State resources but also for creating greater sense of responsibility within the educational system. Howeve such measures will contribute only marginally to the total funding. Th Government and the community in general will find funds for suc programmes as : the universalisation of elementary educatio, liquid ting illiteracy; equality of access to educational opportunities to all sc tions throughout the and functional effectiveness of educational programmes; generating knowledge and developing technologies in scientific fields crucial to self-sustaining economic development; and creating a critical consciousness of the values and imperatives of national survival.

The deleterious consequences of non-investment or inadequate investment in education are indeed very serious. Similarly, the cost of neglecting vocational and technical education and of research is also unacceptable. Sub-optimal performance in these fields could cause irreparable damage to the Indian economy. The network of institutions set up from time to time since Independence to facilitate the application of science and technology would need to be substantially and expeditiously updated, since they are fast becoming obsolete.

In view of these imperatives, education will be treated as a crucial area of investment of national development and survival. The National Policy of Education, 1968, had laid down that the investment on education be gradually increased to reach a level of expenditure of 6 per cent of the national income as early as possible. Since the actual level of investment has remained far short of that target, it is important that greater determination be shown now to find the funds for the programmes laid down in this policy. While the actual requirements will be computed from time to time on the basis of monitoring and review, the outlay on education will be shaped up to the extent essential for policy implementation in the Seventh Plan. It will be ensured that from the Eighth Five-Year Plan onwards it will uniformly exceed to 6 per cent of the National income.

2

COMPARATIVE EDUCATIONAL DATA ON STATES :
Enrolment Ratios and Vocational Facilities

I. States with the Best Positions in Different Areas of Education

1. *States with the highest enrolment ratios in different classes*

(a)	Classes I-V	Tamil Nadu	130.61
(b)	Classes I-V Boys	Sikkim	141.30
(c)	Classes I-V Girls	Tamil Nadu	122.36
(d)	Classes VI-VIII	Kerala	95.57
(c)	Classes VI-VIII Boys	Himachal Pradesh	106.73
(f)	Classes VI-VIII Girls	Kerala	94.30

2. *States with the highest percentage of girls, enrolment to total enrolment in different classes*

(i)	Classes I-V	Meghalaya	49.74
		Kerala	48.79
(ii)	Classes VI-VII	Kerala	49.12
(iii)	Classes IX-X	Kerala	49.63
(iv)	Classes XI-XII	Kerala	43.00

3. *States with the best pupil-teacher ratio (lowest ratio)*

(c)	Primary School	Sikkim	17
(b)	Middle School	Sikkim	15
(c)	High School	Orissa	17
(d)	Higher Secondary/New Pattern	Karnataka	14

4. *States with the highest percentage of trained teachers*

(i)	Primary	Gujarat	100
(ii)	Middle School	1. Gujarat	100
		2. Tamil Nadu	100
(iii)	High School	Haryana	99.6
(iv)	Higher Secondary/New Pattern	1. Karnataka	100
		2. Kerala	100
		3. Orissa	100

II. States with the Most Unfavourable Positions in Different Areas of Education

1. *States with the minimum enrolment ratios in different classes*

	Classes	*State with enrolment ratio*		*All India ratio*
(a)	Classes I-V	Uttar Pradesh	76.22	95.96
(b)	Classes I-V Boys	Jammu & Kashmir	96.06	111.83
(c)	Classes I-V Girls	Rajasthan	46.73	79.21
(d)	Classes VI-VIII	Bihar	31.56	53.14
(e)	Classes VI-VIII Boys	Bihar	47.08	66.5
(f)	Classes VI-VIII Girls	Bihar	15.47	38.95

2. *States with the lowest percentage of girls enrolment to total enrolment in different classes*

(i)	Classes I-V	Rajasthan	28.02	41.16
(ii)	Classes VI-VIII	Rajasthan	19.75	35.45
(iii)	Classes IX X	Rajasthan	16.82	31.74
(iv)	Classes XI-XII	Rajasthan	16.42	30.71

3. *States with the most unfavourable pupil-teacher ratio* (maximum ratio)

(a)	Primary School	Bihar	49
(b)	Middle School	West Bengal	46
(c)	High School	West Bengal	36
(d)	Higher Secondary/ New Pattern	1.Maharashtra	37
		2.Uttar Pradesh	37

4. *States with the most unfavourable position regarding percentage of trained teachers*

(i)	Primary School	Meghalaya	42.0
(ii)	Middle School	Assam	28.0
(iii)	High School/ Post Basic School	Assam	23.0
(iv)	Higher Secondary/ New Pattern	Assam	25.0

III. States with the Highest and the Lowest Enrolment Ratio in Classes I to VIII

Item	*State with highest position*	*State with lowest position*	*India as a whole*
Enrolment: ratios according to selected educational statistics 1986-87, Ministry of Human Resource Development			
1. Classes I-V (age 6-11 years)	Sikkim 128.42 (127.72)	Uttar Pradesh 76.22 (69.29)	95.96 (93.63)
(a) Boys	Sikkim 141.30 (139.40)	Jammu & Kashmir 96.06 (91.35)	111.83 (106.42)
(b) Girls	Tamil Nadu 122.36 (120.01)	Rajashan 46 73 (50.62)	79.21 (79.89)
2. Classes VI-VIII (age 11-14 years)	Kerala 95.57 (88.28)	Bihar 31.56 (29.92)	53.14 (48.51)
(a) Boys	Himachal Pradesh 106.73 (93.07)	Andhra Pradesh 42.22 (48.88)	66.50 (60.61)
(b) Girls	Kerala 94.30 (88.09)	Bihar 15.47 (16.11)	38.95 (35.57)
Gross enrolment ratios according to Fifth All India Educational Survey			
1. Classes I-V (age 6-11 years)	Sikkim (127.72) 128.42	Uttar Pradesh (69.29) 69.29	(93.63) 95.96
(a) Boys	Sikkim (139.40) 141.30	Uttar Pradesh (86.17) 96.49	(106.42) 111.83
(b) Girls	Tamil Nadu (120.01) 122.36	Uttar Pradesh (50.33) 53.41	(79.89) 79.20
2. Classes VI-VIII (age 11-14 years)	Kerala (88.28) 95.57	Bihar (29.92) 31.56	(48.51)
(a) Boys	Himachal Pradesh (93.07) 106.73	Bihar (43.00) 47.08	(60.61) 66.50
(b) Girl	Kerala (88.09) 94.30	Bihar (16.11) 15.7	(35.57) 38.95

Notes : 1. The Ministry of Human Resource Development (Department of Education) Government of India has used the term *Enrolment Ratios* as against *Gross Enrolment Ratios* used in the Fifth All-India Educational Survey, NCERT.

2. Figures in the parentheses are from the Fifth All India Educational Survey and the Parallel figures from the Statistics compiled by the Ministry of Human Resource Development.

IV. States with Maximum and Minimum Vocational Facilities

1. States with maximum vocational facilities

	Item	*State*	*Number*
(a)	Number of institutions	Tamil Nadu	1144
(b)	Number of students	Tamil Nadu	73496
(c)	Number of courses	Maharashtra	46

2. States with minimum vocational facilities

(a)	Number of institutions	Pondicherry	3
(b)	Number of students	Punjab	304
(c)	Number of courses	Uttar Pradesh	1

Note: Only 15 States/Union Territories have provided for vocational courses.

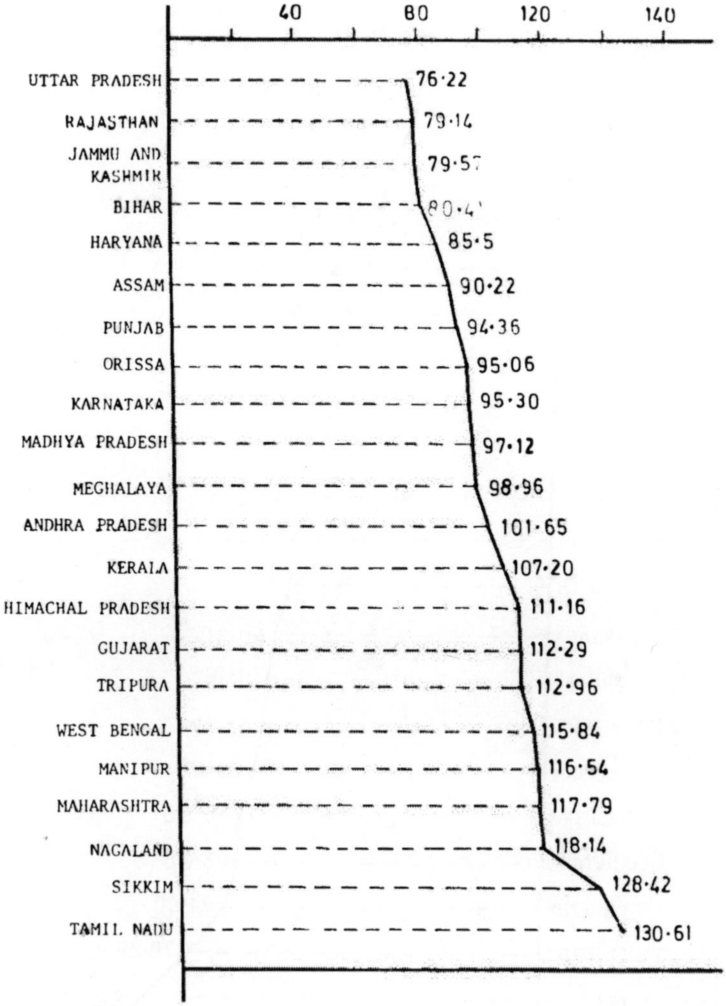

FIG. 2.1: Enrolment Ratio in Classes I to V (General Education)

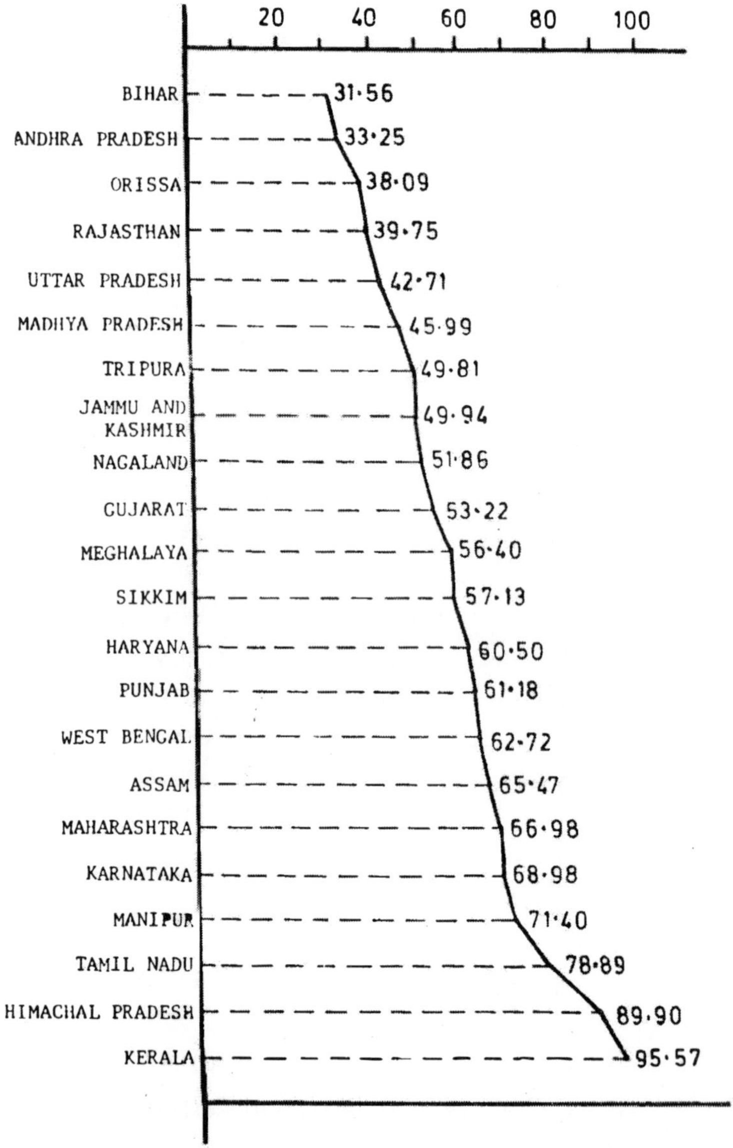

FIG. 2.2: Enrolment Ratio in Classes VI-VIII (General Education)

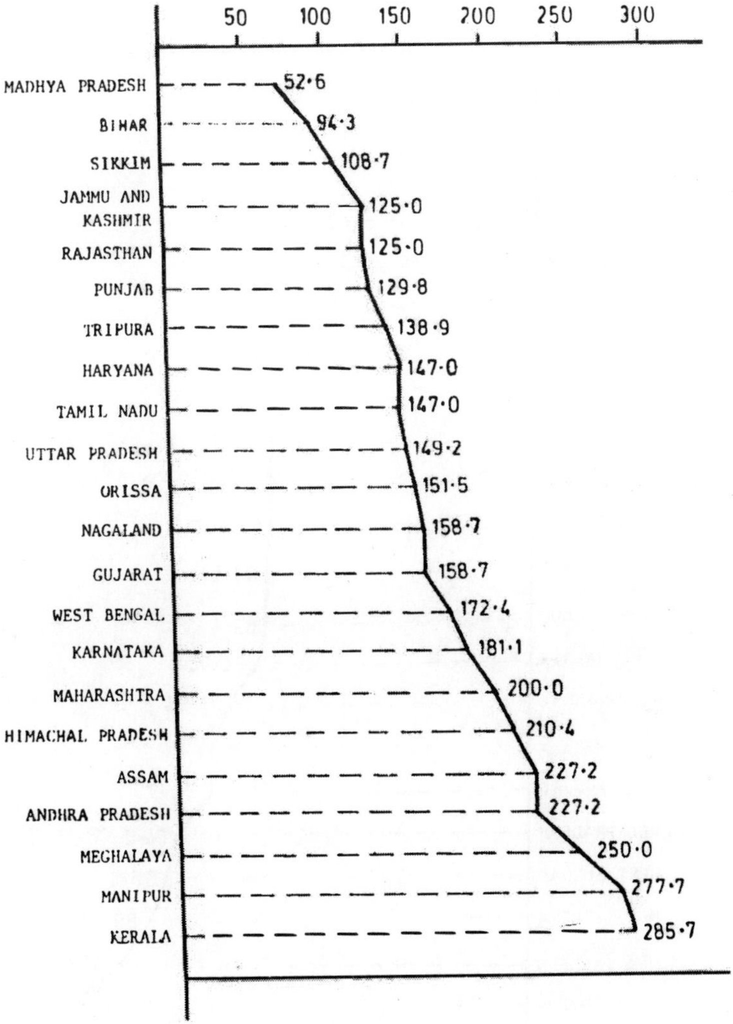

FIG. 2.3: Enrolment at High/Post Basic Stage/Classes Per 10,000 Population (Inhabitants)

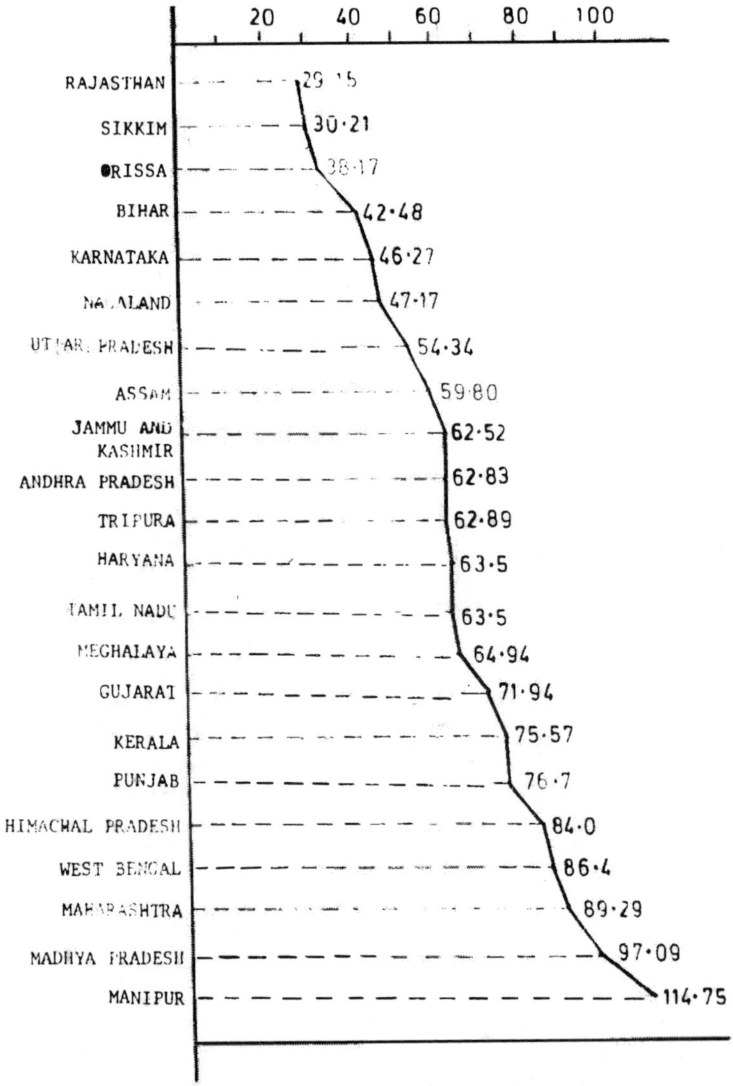

FIG. 2.4: Enrolment at Higher Secondary (Old and New Pattern/Pre University/Intermediate Per 10,000 Inhabitants).

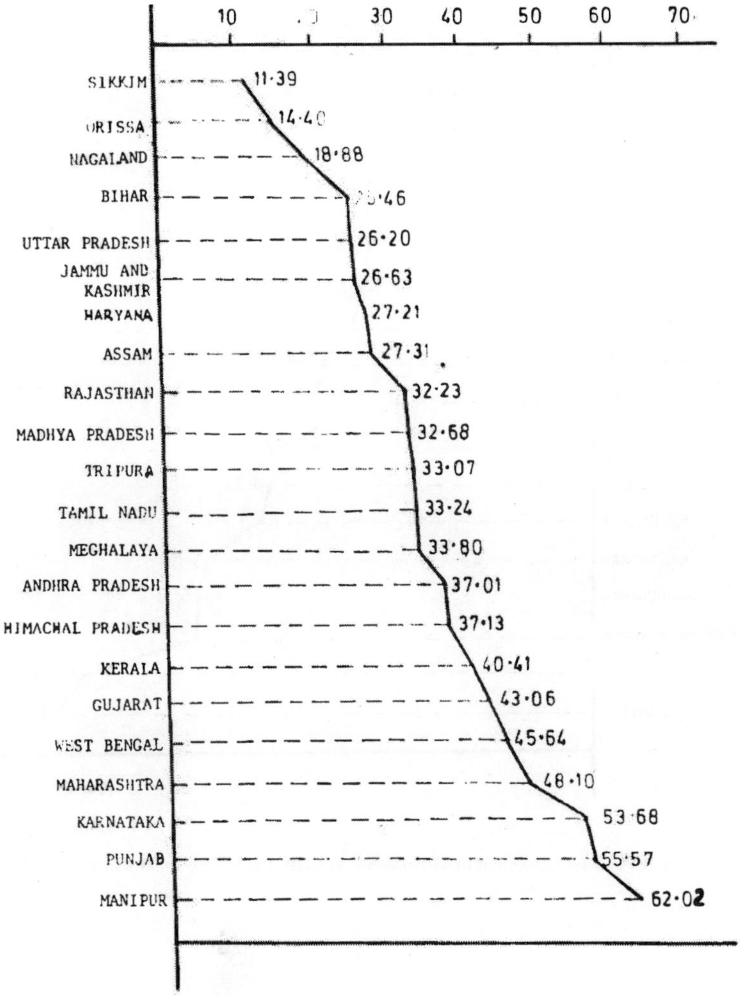

FIG. 2.5: Enrolment in B.A./B.Sc./B.Com. Per 10,000 Population

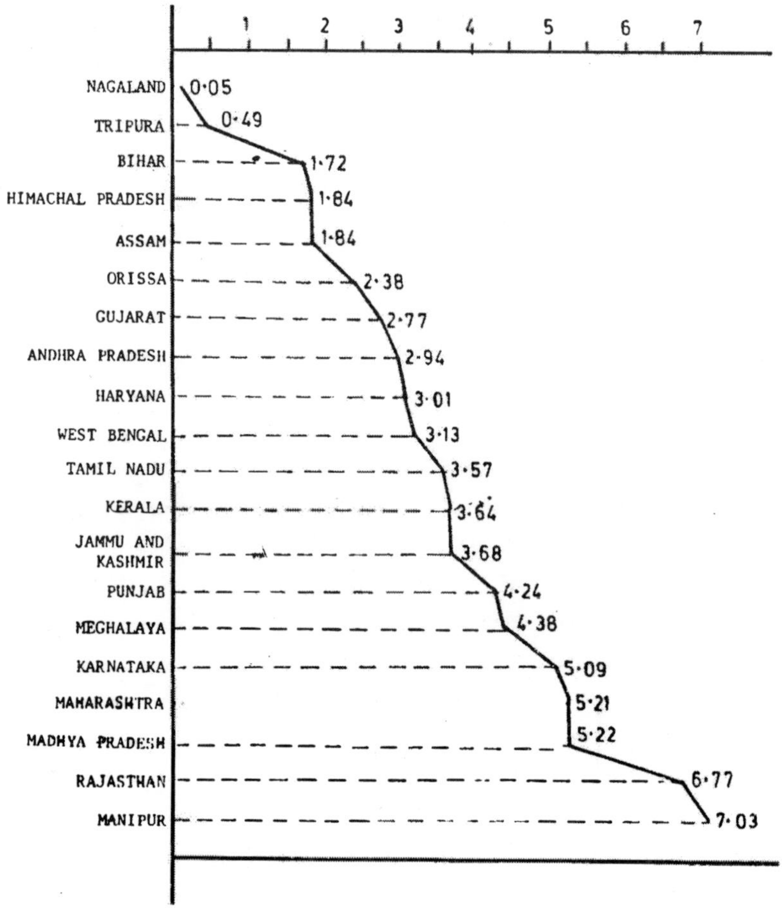

FIG. 2.6: Enrolment in M.A./M.Sc./M.Com. Per 10,000 Inhabitants

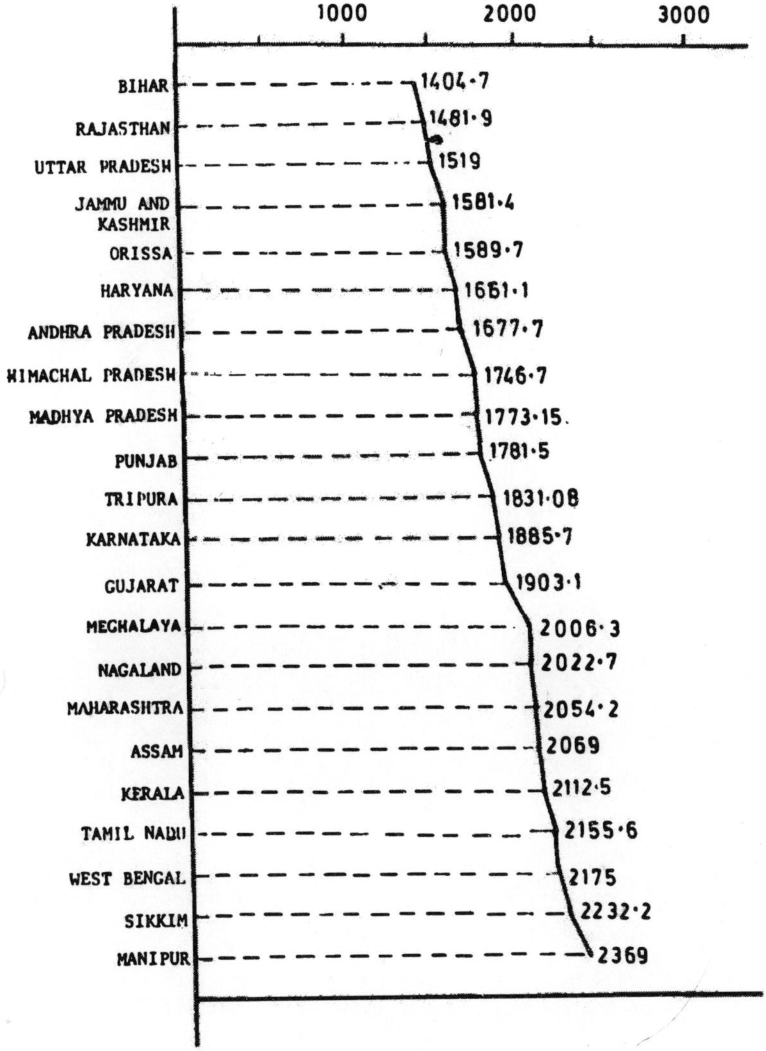

FIG. 2.7: Enrolment Per 10,000 Inhabitants (All Stages)

3

COMPARATIVE EDUCATIONAL DATA ON STATES :

A. States with the Most Favourable Situation Regarding Number of Institutions per 10 lakhs of Inhabitants

Category of Institution	State	Number per 10 lakhs of inhabitants
1. Primary	Meghalaya	2638.5
2. Middle	Gujarat	402.0
3. High	Manipur	211.0
4. Higher Secondary	Tripura	38.6
5. Intermediate	Uttar Pradesh	26.5
6. Arts/Science/Commerce Colleges	Nagaland	15.3
7. Teacher training colleges	Manipur	9.1 per 50 lakhs
8. Universities	Meghalaya	One University per 16 lakhs

B. States with the Most Favourable Situation in Respect of Number of Inhabitants per Institution

Type of Institution	State	No. of inhabitants served by one Institution
1. Primary/Junior Basic	Meghalaya	379
2. Middle/Senior basic	Gujarat	2487
3. High/Post Basic	Manipur	4738
4. Higher Secondary/10+2	Tripura	25873
5. Junior/Intermediate college (only in a few States)	Uttar Pradesh	37682
6. Arts, Science & Commerce College	Nagaland	65480
7. University	Meghalaya	1574900

C. States with the Most Unfavourable Situation in Respect of Number of Inhabitants per Institution

Type of Institution	State	No. of inhabitants served by one institution
1. Primary/Junior Basic	Kerala	4149
2. Middle/Senior Basic	West Bengal	15606
3. High/Post Basic	Nagaland	327400
4. Higher Secondary/10+2	Andhra	1248360
5. Arts, Science and Commerce College	Sikkim	393200
6. University	Rajasthan	8036920 (80 lakhs)

D. **Percentage of Rural Population with Primary Schools/Sections within the Habitation**

Sl.No.	*State/Union Territory*	***Ranking order***
1.	Lakshadweep	100
2.	Nagaland	98.85
3.	Delhi	98.06
4.	Mizoram	98.05
5.	Gujarat	97.83
6.	Chandigarh	96.92
7.	Punjab	96.80
8.	Haryana	96.68
9.	Andhra Pradesh	92.72
10.	Karnataka	92.50
11.	Maharashtra	92.42
12.	Manipur	89.97
13.	Pondicherry	88.54
14.	Kerala	87.67
15.	Rajasthan	86.84
16.	Tamil Nadu	83.92
17.	Assam	81.75
18.	Madhya Pradesh	81.51
19.	Meghalaya	80.87
20.	West Bengal	79.71
21.	Bihar	78.53
22.	Jammu & Kashmir	78.23
23.	Daman & Diu	77.13
24.	Orissa	77.08
25.	Sikkim	72.13
26.	A & N Islands	68.41
27.	Arunachal Pradesh	65.85
28.	Goa	57.72
29.	Tripura	57.04
30.	Uttar Pradesh	55.69
31.	Dadra & Nagar Haveli	50.74
32.	Himachal Pradesh	46.51
	All India	80.34%

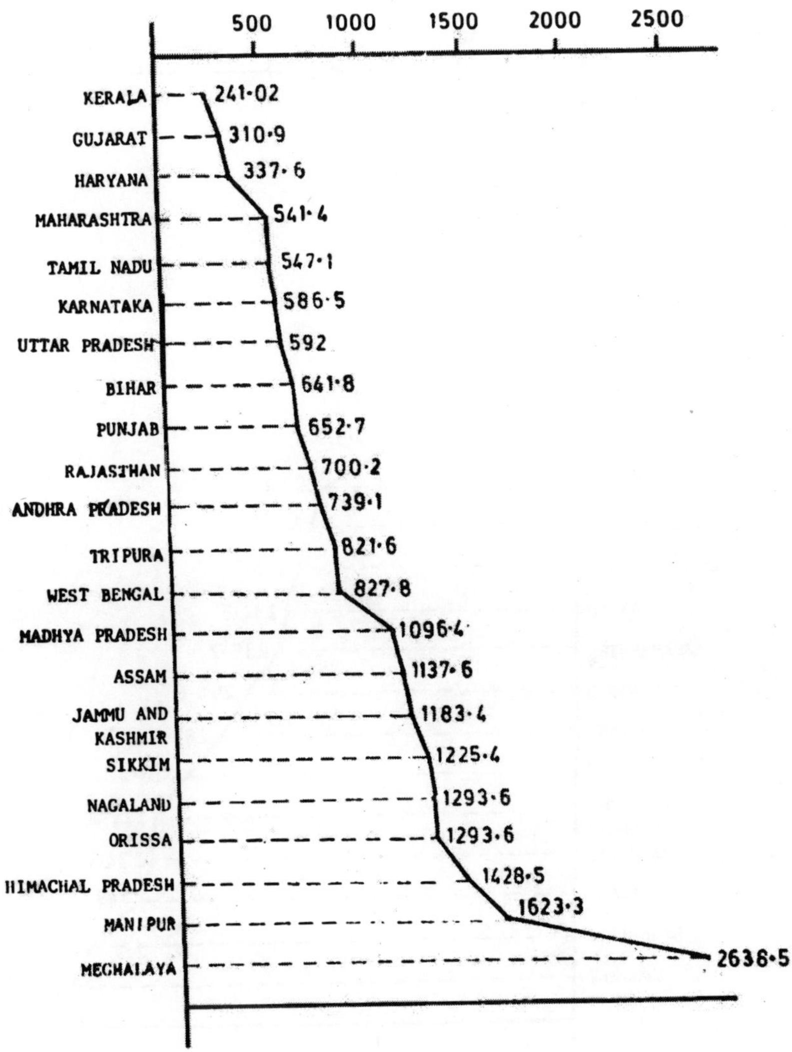

FIG. 3.1: Number of Primary/Junior Basic Schools Per 10 Lakhs of Population

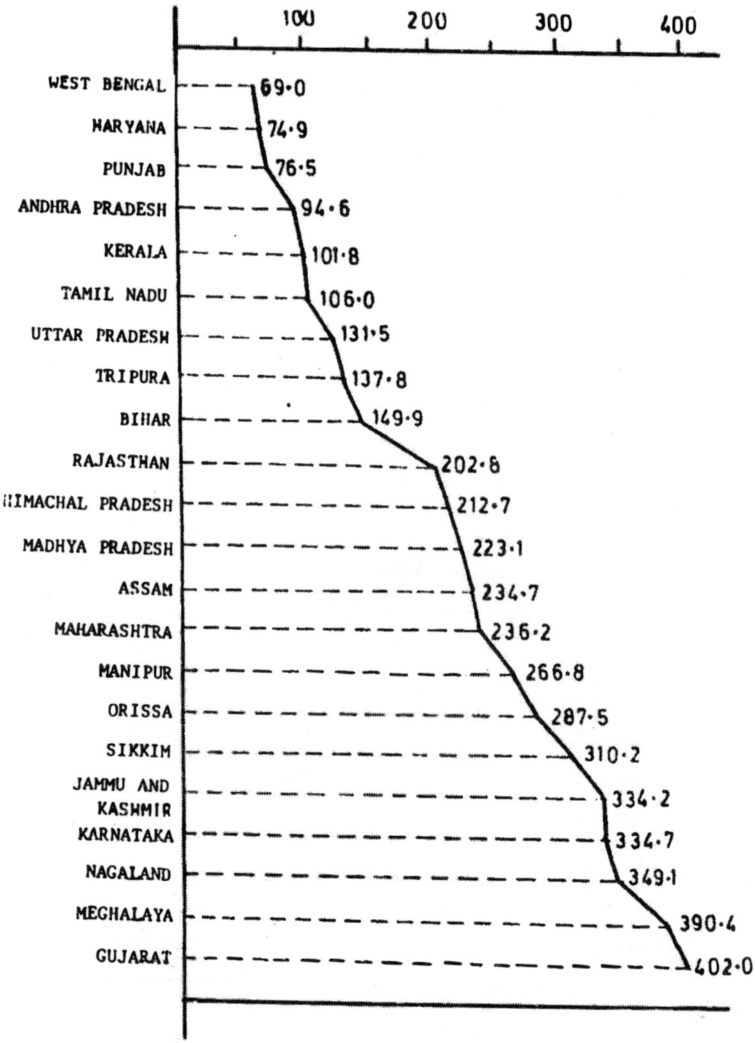

FIG. 3.2: Number of Middle/Senior Basic Schools Per 10 Lakhs of Population

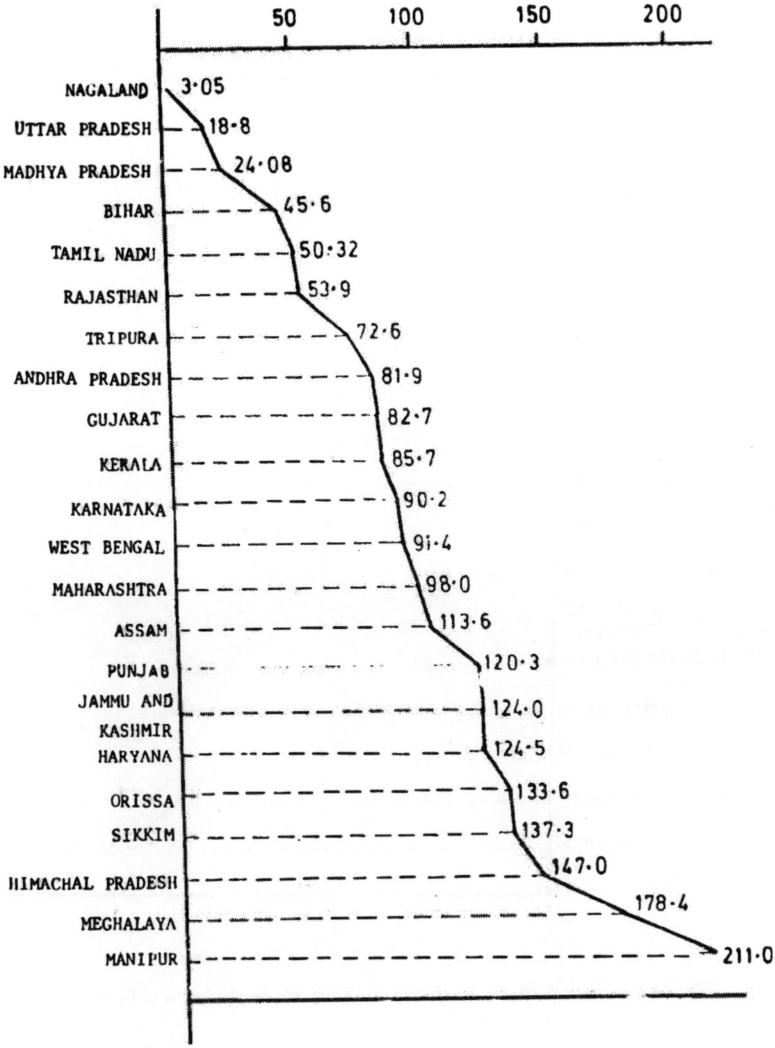

FIG. 3.3: No. of High/Post-Basic Schools Per 10 Lakhs of Population

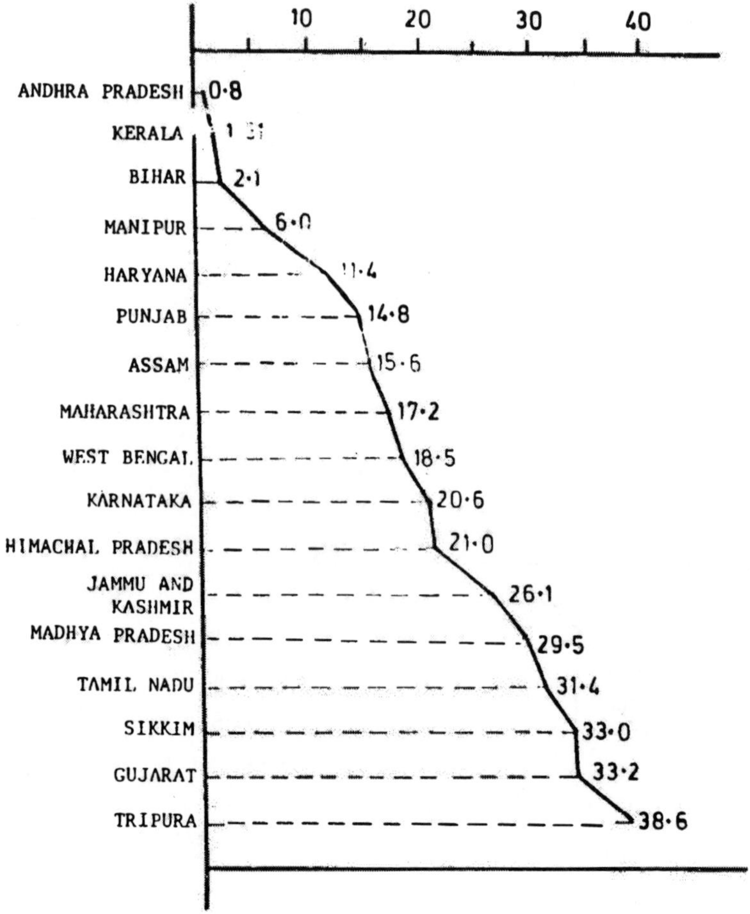

FIG. 3.4 : Number of Higher Secondary 10+2 Schools Per 10 Lakhs of Population

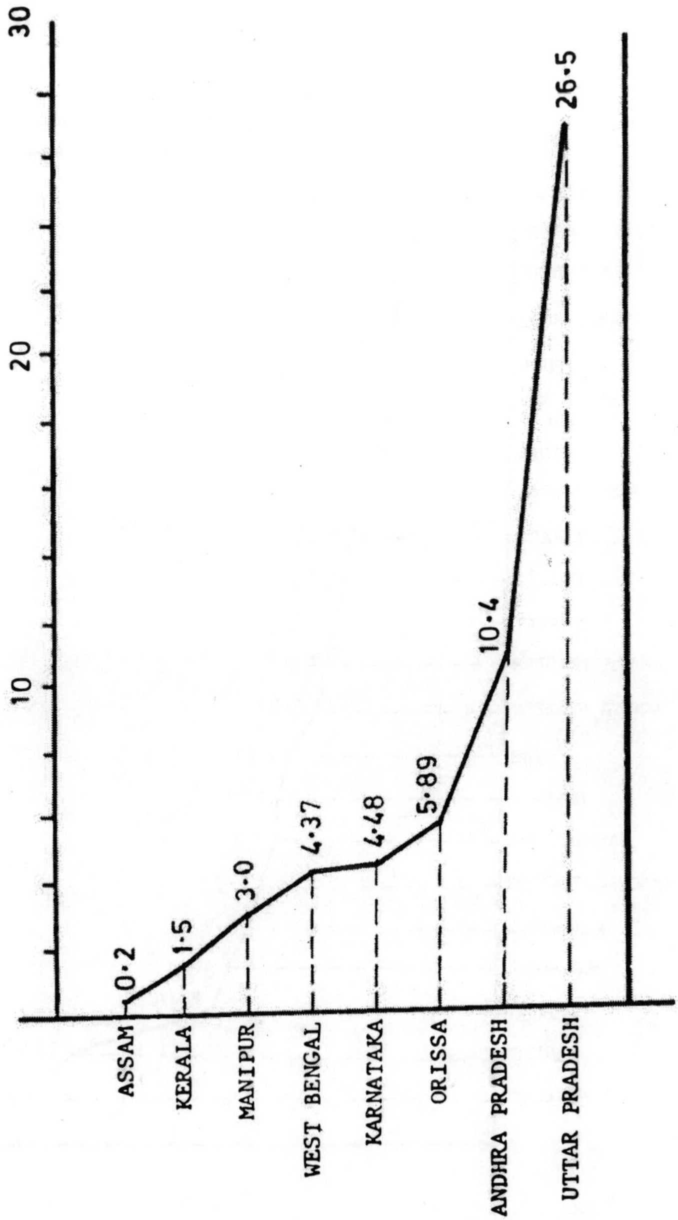

FIG. 3.5: Number of Junior/Intermediate Colleges Per 10 Lakhs of Population

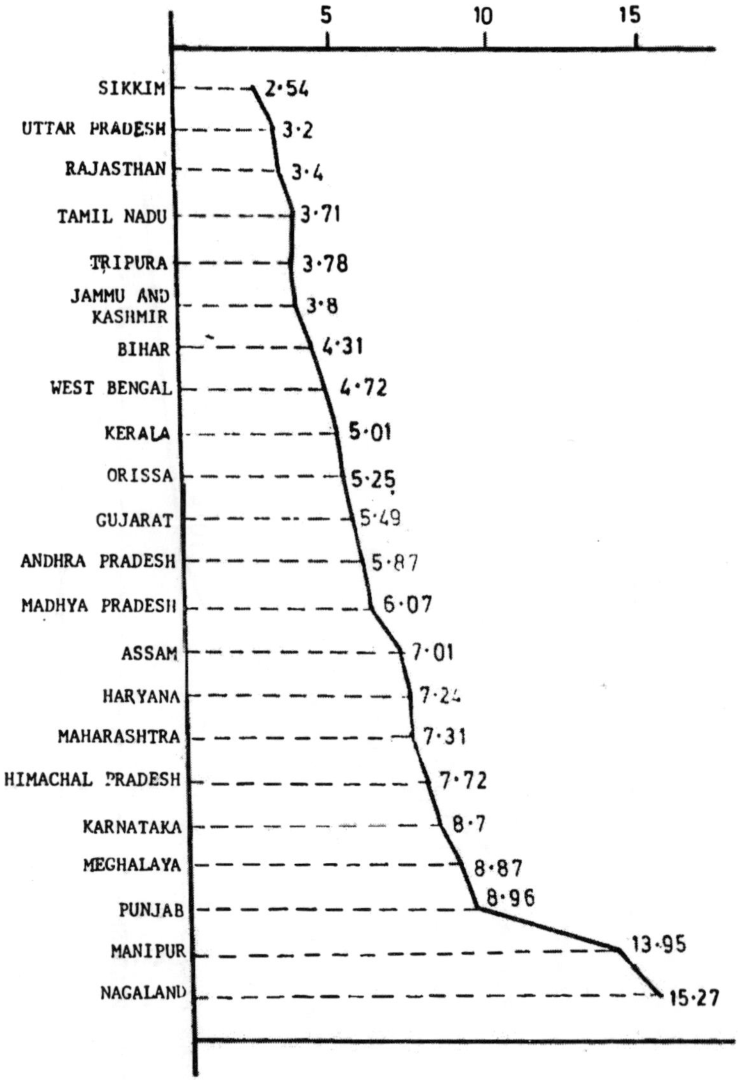

FIG. 3.6: No. of Arts/Science/Commerce Colleges Per 10 Lakhs of Population

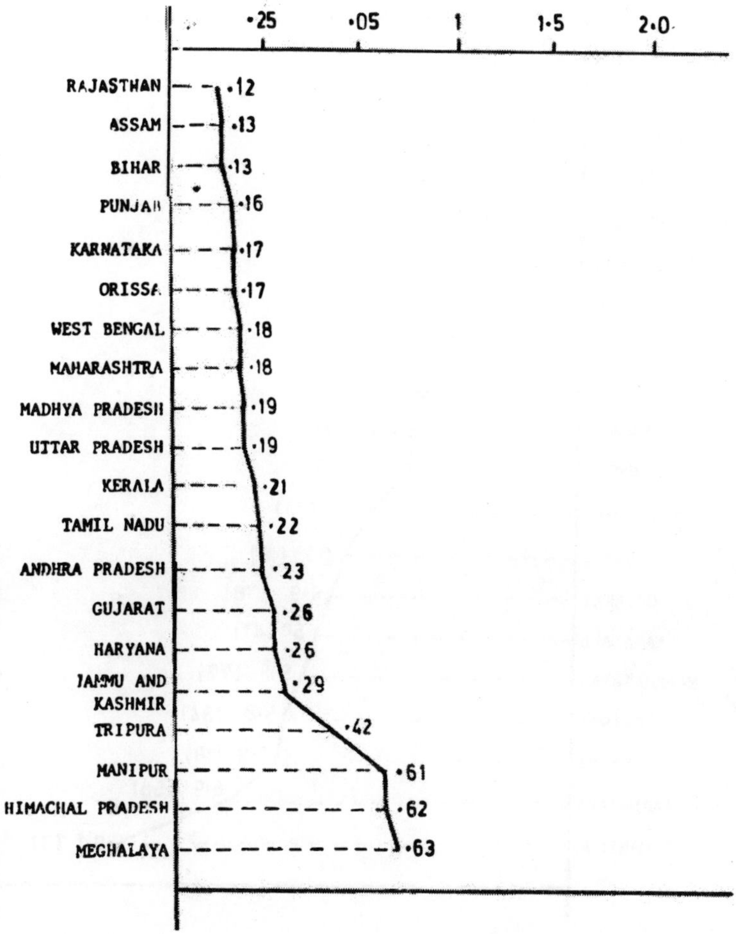

FIG. 3.7: Number of Universities Per 10 Lakhs of Population

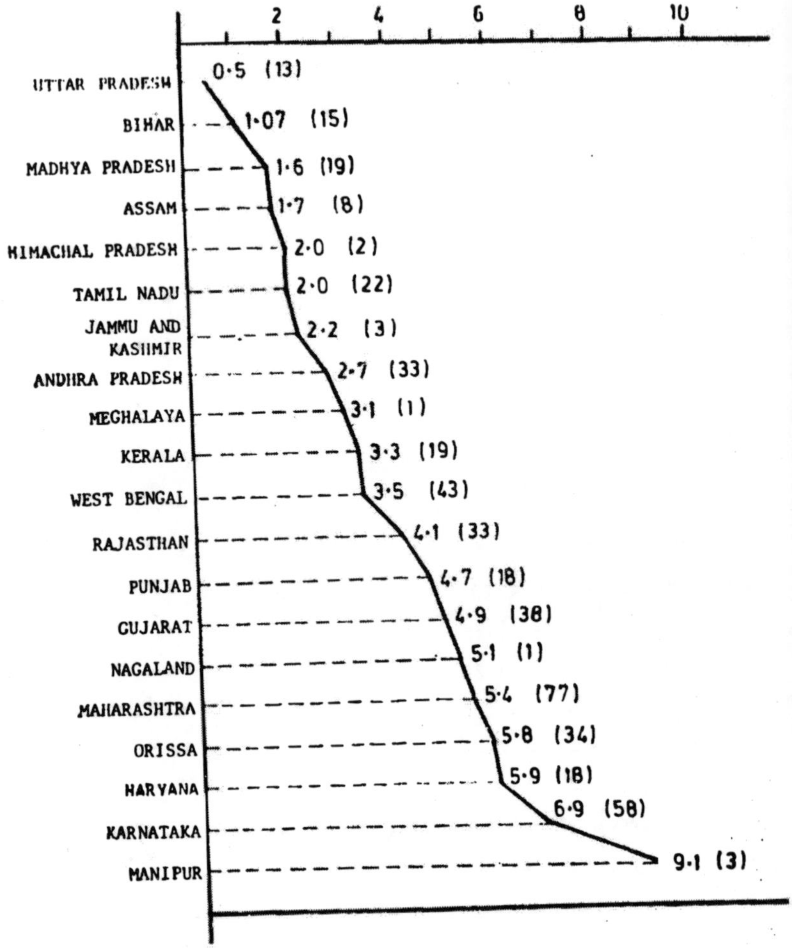

FIG. 3.8: Number of Teachers Traninig Colleges Per 50 Lakhs of Inhabitants
Note : Figures in Parentheses indicate the numbers of Teacher Training Colleges

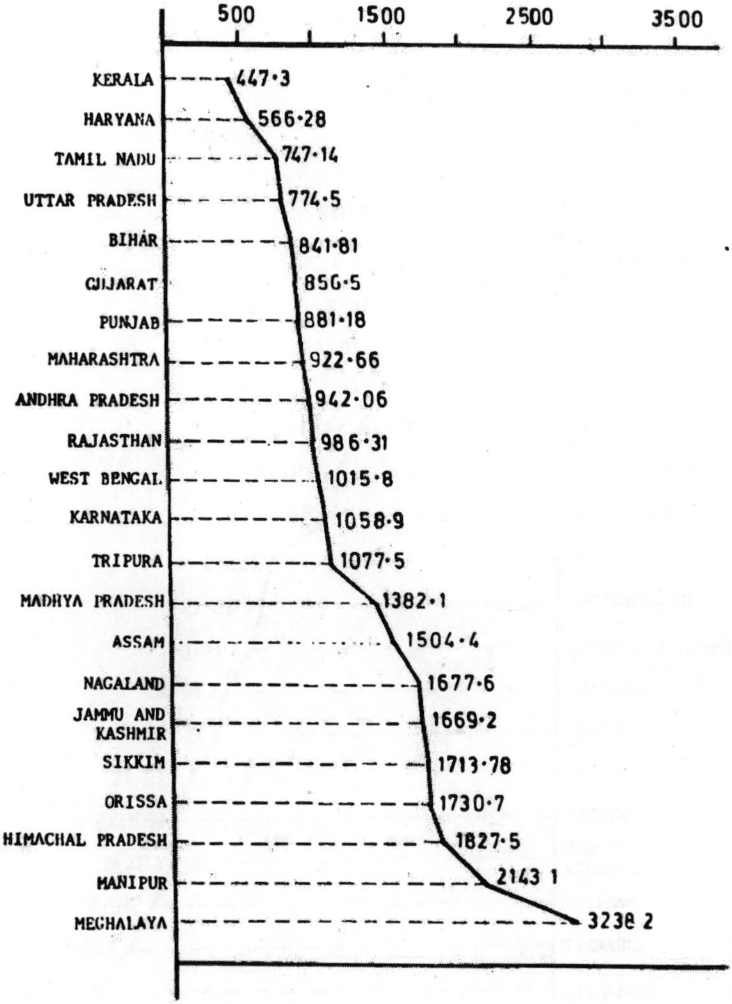

FIG. 3.9: Number of Institutions Per 10 Lakhs of Inhabitants (Excluding Pre Primary)

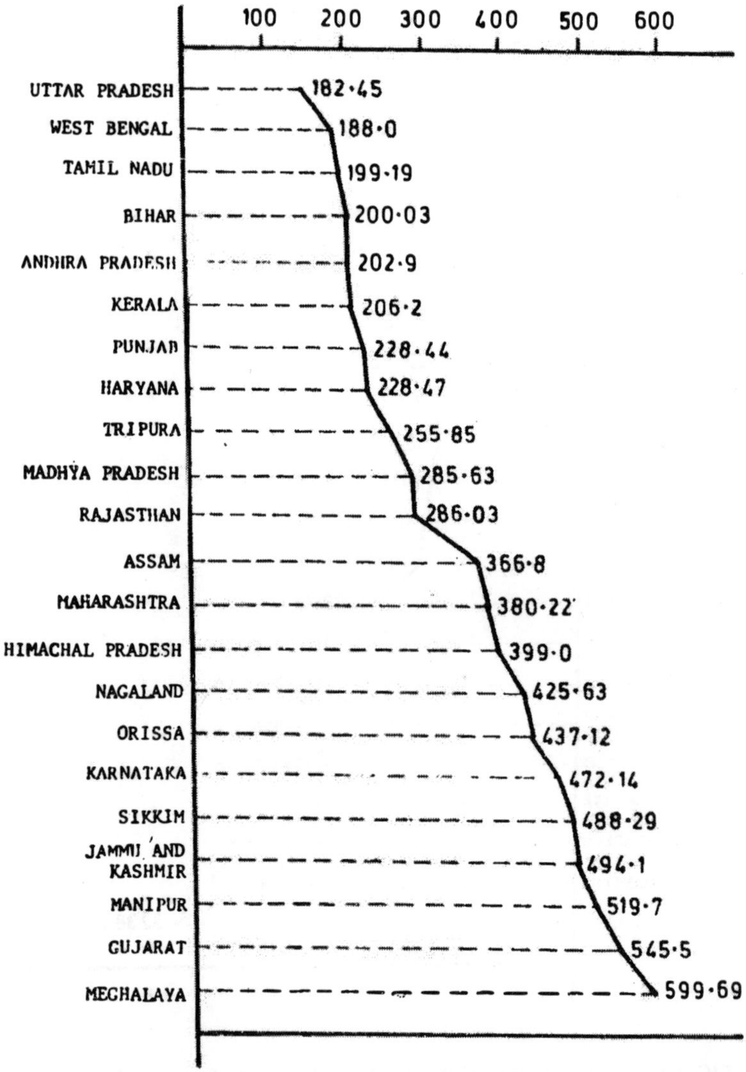

FIG. 3.10: Number of Institutions (Excluding Pre-Primary and Primary) per 10 Lakhs of Inhabitants.

4

COMPARATIVE STUDY OF DIVERSE ISSUES IN EDUCATION IN STATES

TABLE 4.1: **Number of Institutions offering Vocational Courses at +2 Stage and Enrolment**

Sl. No.	*State/ Union Territory*	*No. of Institu-tions*	*No. of Courses*	*Class XI*		*Class XII*	
				Boys/ Girls	*Total*	*Boys/ Girls*	*Total*
1.	Tamil Nadu	1144	26	20257 20004	40261	19676 13559	33235
2.	Maharashtra	91	46	6918 1032	7950	5343 802	6145
3.	Gujarat	45	14	3654 2374	6028	4280 2520	6800
4.	Karnataka	105	29	3538 1020	4558	2815 546	3361
5.	Haryana	41	19	1673 225	1898	1649 278	1927
6.	Kerala	53	11	845 667	1515	756 574	1330
7.	Delhi	52	21	776 702	1478	354 640	994
8.	Madhya Pradesh	11	18	706 335	1041	11 30	41
9.	Uttar Pradesh	41	1	1025 0	1025	675 0	675
10.	West Bengal	90	4	793 46	839	749 34	789
11.	Orissa	02	3	294 121	415	226 103	329
12.	Rajasthan	10	11	263 107	370	2273 65	2378
13.	Pondicherry	3	8	225 102	327	183 78	261
14.	Punjab	13	10	286 18	304	Nil	Nil
15.	Goa	4	3	65 89	154	80 80	160
	All India	1706		41318 26862	68180	39070 19321	58391

Grand Total Classes XI-XIII = 1,26,571

TABLE 4.2: **States with the Best (Lowest) and Unfavourable (Maximum) Pupil-Teacher Ratio**

Class/Stage	*State with Best Position*	*State with Most Unfavourable Position*	*All India Average*
Primary School/ Stage	Sikkim 17 (15)	Andhra 56 (44)	42 (44)
Middle School/Stage	Sikkim 15 (17)	West Bengal 46 (41)	35 (29)
High School/ Secondary Stage	Orissa 17 (12)	West Bengal 36 (15)	29 21
Higher Secondary School/Stage (New Pattern)	Karnataka 14 (21)	Maharashtra 37 (53) Uttar Pradesh 37 (26)	29 (15)
Position in accordance with Fifth All India Survey			
Primary School/ Stage	Sikkim (15)	Gujarat (61)	
Middle School/Stage	Sikkim (17) 15	West Bengal (41) 46	
High School/ Secondary Stage	Orissa (12) 17	Gujarat (32) 24	
Higher Secondary/ School/Stage (New Pattern)	Punjab (4) 26	Maharashtra (53) 37	

TABLE 4.3: **Pupil-Teacher Ratio at Various Stages in States**

State/Union Territory	*Primary School/ Junior Basic*	*Middle Senior Basic School*	*High/Post-Basic School*	*Higher Secondary/ Junior College/ 10+2*
Andhra Pradesh	56(44)	44(24)	33(21)	16(28)
Assam	43(30)	34(30)	27(23)	19(30)
Bihar	49(60)	41(25)	34(24)	34(18)
Gujarat	41(61)	40(21)	24(32)	28(13)
Haryana	40(53)	33(40)	31(10)	25(10)
Himachal Pradesh	38(38)	19(29)	30(18)	18(11)
Jammu & Kashmir	31(33)	24(19)	18(12)	17(13)
Karnataka	40(48)	45(33)	34(27)	14(21)
Kerala	32(40)	29(30)	27(18)	25(11)
Madhya Pradesh	44(39)	29(29)	27(28)	18(6)
Maharashtra	38(42)	39(37)	31(23)	37(53)
Manipur	20(17)	18(16)	21(13)	17(5)
Meghalaya	31(37)	16(21)	25(14)	--
Nagaland	23(20)	21(15)	20(8)	--
Orissa	38(39)	31(31)	17(12)	--(9)
Punjab	39(40)	18(39)	24(11)	26(4)
Rajasthan	45(55)	30(18)	20(18)	--(6)
Sikkim	17(15)	15(17)	19(9)	15(7)
Tamil Nadu	44(56)	44(37)	30(27)	30(7)
Tripura	40(36)	30(29)	28(13)	22(6)
Uttar Pradesh	48(41)	26(35)	35(27)	37(26)
West Bengal	39(41)	46(41)	36(15)	31(13)
Andaman & Nicobar Islands	21(31)	19(26)	23(11)	22(9)
Arunachal Pradesh	31(34)	23(17)	23(14)	20(5)
Chandigarh	20(28)	31(31)	24(15)	--(07)
Dadra and Nagar Haveli	82(35)	11(27)	42(36)	20(07)
Delhi	36(34)	19(31)	26(18)	22(11)
Goa, Daman & Diu	26(41)	24(36)	30(26)	31(25)
Lakshadweep	27(28)	29(18)	07(14)	16
Mizoram	24(27)	15(13)	15(16)	--(13)
Pondicherry	30(34)	31(29)	27(17)	34(23)
INDIA	42(44)	35(29)	29(21)	29(15)

Notes: 1. Figures compiled by the Ministry of Human Resource Development and the NCERT in the Fifth All India Educational Survey do not agree. The Ministry has used the term Pupil-Teacher Ratio at the School whereas NCERT at the Stage.

2. Figures in parentheses have been taken from the Fifth All India Educational Survey.

All India Figures are as under

School/Stage	*Figures compiled by the Ministry*	*Figures compiled by NCERT*
1. Primary School/Stage	42	44
2. Middle School/Stage	35	29
3. High School/Secondary Stage	29	21
4. Higher Secondary/ New Pattern/Higher Secondary Stage	29	15

TABLE 4.4: **Percentage of Trained Teachers at Various Levels in States**

State/Union Territory	*Primary/ Junior Basic School*	*Middle/ Senior Basic School*	*High/Post-Basic/ Secondary School*	*Higher Secondary/ New Pattern*
Andhra Pradesh	95.9	96.5	99.0	99.7
Assam	65.0	28.0	23.0	25.0
Bihar	92.9	91.6	95.8	96.3
Gujarat	100.0	100.0	99.0	98.0
Haryana	100.0	99.0	99.6	89.9
Himachal Pradesh	97.2	99.3	97.8	75.0
Jammu & Kashmir	80.0	80.0	79.0	85.0
Karnataka	89.0	92.0	93.0	100.0
Kerala	96.0	92.0	98.0	100.0
Madhya Pradesh	NA	NA	NA	NA
Maharashtra	99.0	95.0	95.0	95.0
Manipur	67.0	51.0	33.0	56.5
Meghalaya	42.0	31.0	30.0	—
Nagaland	86.2	48.7	62.4	—
Orissa	91.8	61.0	75.0	100.0
Punjab	99.3	98.0	99.1	99.7
Rajasthan	85.3	92.8	96.6	—
Sikkim	53.0	39.0	42.3	42.1
Tamil Nadu	100.0	100.0	97.0	98.0
Tripura	49.5	55.8	53.0	68.3
Uttar Pradesh	95.0	93.0	96.8	95.0
West Bengal	56.0	58.0	77.0	71.0
Andaman & Nicobar Islands	95.2	95.5	94.7	95.8
Arunachal Pradesh	40.0	42.7	53.6	49.5
Chandigarh	100.0	100.0	100.0	—
Dadra & Nagar Haveli	97.8	91.7	97.4	85.0
Delhi	100.0	98.0	99.0	98.0
Goa, Daman & Diu	92.0	92.0	83.0	66.0
Lakshadweep	97.0	96.0	98.0	100.0
Mizoram	51.0	51.1	40.6	—
Pondicherry	100.0	100.0	100.0	100.0
INDIA	87.26	89.6	89.6	90.2

TABLE 4.5: **Secondary Teacher Training Institutions Statewise and University-wise**

A. *University Departments of Education, Number of Colleges of Education and other Colleges with B.Ed. etc.: State-wise and University-wise*

State/University	*University Depart—ment of Education*	*Colleges of Educa—cation*	*Other Colleges with B.Ed. etc.*	*Total Colleges*
1	2	3	4	5
Andhra Pradesh				
1. Andhra	1	9	—	10
2. Kakati, Warrangal	1	1	—	2
3. Nagarjuna	—	8	—	8
4. Osmania	1	7	—	8
5. Sri Venkateshwara Tirupati	—	9	1	10
Assam				
6. Dibrugarh	1	2	—	3
7 Gauhati	1	8	—	9
Bihar				
8. Bhagalpur	—	2	—	2
9. Bihar	—	3	—	3
9(a) L.N.Mithila, Darbhanga	—	3	—	3
10. Magadh	—	2	—	2
11. Patna	1	3	—	4
12. Ranchi	—	5	—	5
Goa				
13. Goa	—	1	—	1
Gujarat				
14. Baroda	1	—	—	1
15. Bhan Nagar	1	1	—	2
16. Gujarat, Ahmedabad	1	20	—	21
17. Gujarat, Vidyapith	1	1	—	2
18. M.S. Baroda	1	—	—	1
19. Sardar Vallabh Vidya Nagar	—	5	—	5
20. Saurashtra (Rajkot)	1	6	—	7
21. South Gujarat (Surat)	—	2	—	2
Haryana				
22. Kurukshetra	1	6	—	7
23. M.D. Rohtak	1	13	—	14
Himachal Pradesh				
24. H.P., Shimla	2	1	—	3

TABLE 4-5 (*Contd*)

1	2	3	4	5
Jammu & Kashmir				
25. Jammu	1	3	—	4
26. Kashmir, Srinagar	1	1	2	4
Karnataka				
27. Bangalore	1	16	—	17
28. Gulbarga	—	7	—	7
29. Karnataka, Dharwad	1	8	—	9
30. Mysore	1	18	—	19
Kerala				
31. Calicut	1	5	—	6
32. Gandhiji, Kottayam	—	7	—	7
33. Kerala	1	9	—	10
Madhya Pradesh				
34. Awadesh Pratap, Rewa	—	2	4	6
35. Bhopal	1	4	4	9
36. Bilaspur	—	1	—	1
37. Devi Ahliya, Indore	1	—	1	1
38. H.S. Gaur	1	3	1	5
39. Guru Ghasidas, Bilaspur	—	3	3	6
40. Jabalpur	—	3	3	6
41. Jiwaji, Gwalior	—	1	—	1
42. Ravi Shankar, Raipur	1	2	—	3
43. Vikram (Ujjain)	—	4	—	4
Maharashtra				
44. Amravati	—	4	—	4
45. Bombay	1	19	—	20
46. Marathwada, Aurangabad	—	13	—	13
47. Nagpur	1	7	—	8
48. Poona	—	11	—	11
49. Shivaji, Kolhapur	—	11	—	11
50. S.N.D.T. Women, Bombay	—	2	—	2
Manipur				
51. Manipur	—	1	—	1
Meghalaya				
52. North-East Hill, Shillong	—	3	1	4
Orissa				
53. Berhampur	—	7	—	7
54. Sambalpur	—	8	—	8
55. Utkal (Correspondence also)	1	14	2	17

TABLE 4-5 (*Contd*)

1	2	3	4	5
Punjab				
56. Guru Nanak Dev, Amritsar	—	7	—	7
57. Panjab, Chandigarh	—	13	—	13
58. Punjab Agricultural, Ludhiana	—	1	—	1
59. Punjabi, Patiala	1	3	—	4
Rajasthan				
60. Banasthali Vidya Pith	—	1	—	1
61. Jodhpur	—	1	—	1
62. Rajasthan, Jaipur (Correspondence also)	1	35	—	36
63. Mohan Lal Sukhadia (Udaipur)	—	3	—	3
Tamil Nadu				
64. Alagapa	—	1	—	1
65. Annamalai (Correspondence also)	1	1	—	2
66. Avinashilingam, Coimbatore	—	—	1	1
67. Bharathiar, Coimbatore	—	3	—	3
68. Bharathi Dasam Tiruchirapalli	—	2	—	2
69. Dakshin Bharat Hindi Prachar Sabha, Madras	—	5	—	5
70. Madras	1	9	—	10
71. Madurai, Kamraj	1	10	—	11
Uttar Pradesh				
72. Agra	—	—	8	9
73. Aligarh	1	—	—	1
74. Allahabad	1	—	—	1
75. Avadh	—	—	9	9
76. Banaras	1	2	—	3
77. Bundelkhand, Jhansi	—	—	5	5
78. Dayal Bagh	—	1	1	2
79. Garhwal	1	1	4	6
80. Gorakhpur	1	26	—	27
81. Kanpur	1	18	—	19
82. Kumaon	1	2	—	3
83. Lucknow	1	—	5	6
84. Meerut	1	—	9	10
85. Rohelkhand	—	—	10	10
86. Sampurna Nand Sanskrit, Varanasi	—	—	1	1
West Bengal				
87. Burdwan	—	7	2	9
88. Calcutta	1	13	7	21

TABLE 4-5 (*Contd.*)

1	2	3	4	5
89. Jadavpur	—	2	—	2
90. Kalyani	1	6	—	7
91. North Bengal	—	3	1	4
92. Viswa Bharti	—	1	—	1
Union Territories				
Chandigarh				
93. Punjab	1	1	—	2
Delhi				
94. Delhi	1	—	1	2
95. Jamia Millia	1	—	—	1
96. Lal Bahadur Shastri R.S.K. Vidya Pith, Delhi	—	1	—	1
Total	49	494	86	629

(*Contd.*)

B. State wise Secondary Teacher Education Institutions

Sl.No.	*Name of the State*	*No. of Colleges of Education, B.Ed/B.T. Classes attached and University Departments of Education with B.Ed.*
1.	Andhra Pradesh	38
2.	Assam	12
3.	Bihar	19
4.	Goa	1
5.	Gujarat	41
6.	Haryana	21
7.	Himachal Pradesh	3
8.	Jammu & Kashmir	8
9.	Karnataka	52
10.	Kerala	23
11.	Madhya Pradesh	42
12.	Maharashtra	69
13.	Manipur	1
14.	Meghalaya	4
15.	Orissa	32
16.	Punjab	25
17.	Rajasthan	41
18.	Tamil Nadu	35
19.	Uttar Pradesh	112
20.	West Bengal	44
Union Territories		
1.	Chandigarh	2
2.	Delhi	4
	Total	629

TABLE 4.6: **Per Capita Budgeted Expenditure on Education: State-wise Ranking**

Rank	*State/Union Territory*	*Per Capita Budgeted Expenditure on Education (in Rs.)*
1.	Lakshadweep	602.27
2.	Andaman & Nicobar Islands	366.81
3.	Sikkim	351.98
4.	Nagaland	321.42
5.	Mizoram	308.79
6.	Arunachal Prades	279.53
7.	Goa, Daman & Diu	274.53
8.	Pondicherry	272.57
9.	Manipur	245.38
10.	Himachal Pradesh	213.54
11.	Delhi	200.63
12.	Tripura	196.15
13.	Kerala	180.39
14.	Jammu & Kashmir	175.15
15.	Meghalaya	162.93
16.	Chandigarh	162.57
17.	Dadra & Nagar Haveli	154.80
18.	Gujarat	153.17
19.	Punjab	150.57
20.	Maharashtra	135.79
21.	Andhra Pradesh	132.63
22.	Haryana	128.78
23.	Assam	125.01
24.	Karnataka	124.04
25.	Tamil Nadu	121.87
26.	West Bengal	112.97
27.	Rajasthan	103.16
28.	Orissa	88.33
29.	Madhya Pradesh	87.35
30.	Uttar Pradesh	72.75
31.	Bihar	63.03
	India	112.77

TABLE 4.7 : **Percentage of Budgeted Expenditure on Education to Total Budget (Revenue Account): State-wise Ranking**

Rank	*State/Union Territory*	*Budgeted Expenditure. (Revenue Account in Rs. crores)*			*Percentage*
		Plan	*Non-Plan*	*Total*	
1.	Kerala	36.71	474.34	511.05	33.6
2.	Delhi	32.82	125.87	158.69	33.4
3.	Tamil Nadu	119.52	531.41	650.93	26.6
4.	Rajasthan	38.61	375.93	414.53	26.4
5.	West Bengal	107.68	585.67	693.35	26.2
6.	Assam	67.42	217.84	285.26	25.9
7.	Manipur	6.40	34.06	40.46	25.8
8.	Chandigarh	1.20	8.84	10.05	25.7
9.	Bihar	62.33	437.59	499.92	25.4
10.	Gujarat	112.47	476.15	588.00	25.4
11.	Punjab	19.66	264.49	284.15	24.7
12.	Andhra Pradesh	116.69	678.07	794.76	24.5
13.	Karnataka	32.48	490.61	523.09	23.0
14.	Uttar Pradesh	117.86	794.98	912.84	22.1
15.	Goa, Daman & Diu	5.47	28.95	34.42	21.7
16.	Haryana	33.34	162.37	195.71	21.6
17.	Maharashtra	70.18	895.57	965.75	21.2
18.	Orissa	41.56	217.76	259.32	21.1
19.	Pondicherry	4.93	13.94	18.87	20.8
20.	Himachal Pradesh	13.05	89.18	102.23	20.6
21.	Madhya Pradesh	50.07	468.69	518.76	20.3
22.	Tripura	11.85	34.84	46.69	19.4
23.	Jammu & Kashmir	24.30	95.60	119.90	19.1
24.	Dadra & Nagar Haveli	0.59	1.28	1.87	18.7
25.	Sikkim	6.05	7.79	13.84	17.6
26.	Meghalaya	3.83	21.83	25.66	15.7
27.	Mizoram	4.86	14.35	19.21	14.9
28.	Arunachal Pradesh	6.58	14.29	20.87	13.8
29.	Nagaland	4.23	27.34	31.57	13.8
30.	Andaman and Nicobar Islands	1.21	7.92	9.13	12.9
31.	Lakshadweep	0.59	2.06	2.65	12.7
	India	1154.55	7599.61	8754.16	23.8

TABLE 4.8: **Number and Percentage of One Teacher School — Statewise**

Sl.No.	*State/Union Territory*	*Number*	*Percentage*
1.	Dadra & Nagar Haveli	83	66.94
2.	Karnataka	14350	62.33
3.	Jammu & Kashmir	4380	58.63
4.	Arunachal Pradesh	526	55.25
5.	Rajasthan	15352	54.63
6.	Meghalaya	1969	53.33
7.	Maharashtra	16660	43.73
8.	Orissa	14112	41.29
9.	Gujarat	4784	37.64
10.	Madhya Pradesh	22163	34.58
11.	Assam	8903	34.41
12.	Andhra Pradesh	13217	29.37
13.	Himachal Pradesh	1951	28.26
14.	Bihar	13303	25.89
15.	Pondicherry	75	22.12
16.	Andaman & Nicobar Islands	41	23.16
17.	Manipur	510	18.50
18.	Goa	167	16.82
19.	Mizoram	119	11.84
20.	Uttar Pradesh	8891	11.77
21.	Punjab	1457	11.35
22.	Daman & Diu	3	9.38
23.	Tamil Nadu	2724	9.31
24.	Haryana	382	7.88
25	Tripura	145	7.52
26	Lakshadweep	1	5.56
27	Sikkim	21	4.49
28.	Nagaland	42	3.71
29.	West Bengal	1679	3.46
30.	Chandigarh	1	2.27
31.	Kerala	19	0.31
32.	Delhi	3	0.16
	All India	148033	27.96

TABLE 4.9: **Literacy Rates of States/Union Territories**

Sl. No.	*State/Union Territories*	*1971*			*1981*		
		Persons	*Males*	*Females*	*Persons*	*Males*	*Females*
1.	Kerala	60.42	66.62	54.31	70.74	75.26	65.73
2.	Tamil Nadu	39.46	51.78	26.86	46.76	58.26	34.99
3.	Maharashtra	39.18	51.04	26.43	47.18	58.79	34.79
4.	Gujarat	35.79	46.11	24.75	43.70	54.44	32.30
5.	Punjab	33.67	40.38	25.90	40.86	47.16	33.69
6.	West Bengal	33.20	42.81	22.42	40.94	50.67	30.25
7.	Manipur	32.91	46.04	19.53	41.35	53.29	29.06
8.	Himachal Pradesh	31.96	43.19	20.23	42.48	53.19	31.46
9.	Karnataka	31.52	41.62	20.97	38.46	48.81	27.71
10.	Tripura	30.98	40.20	21.19	42.12	51.70	32.0
11.	Meghalaya	29.49	34.12	24.56	34.08	37.89	30.08
12.	Assam	28.15	36.68	18.63	NA	NA	NA
13.	Nagaland	27.40	35.02	18.65	42.57	50.05	33.89
14.	Haryana	26.89	37.29	14.89	36.14	48.20	22.37
15.	Orissa	26.18	38.29	13.92	34.23	47.10	21.12
16.	Andhra Pradesh	24.57	33.18	15.75	29.94	39.26	20.39
17.	Madhya Pradesh	22.14	32.70	10.92	27.87	39.49	15.53
18.	Uttar Pradesh	21.70	31.50	10.55	27.16	38.76	14.04
19.	Bihar	19.94	30.64	8.72	26.20	38.11	13.62
20.	Rajasthan	19.07	28.74	8.46	24.38	36.30	11.42
21.	Jammu & Kashmir	18.58	26.75	9.28	26.69	36.29	15.88
22.	Sikkim	17.74	25.37	8.90	34.05	43.95	22.20
Union Territories							
1.	Chandigarh	61.56	66.97	54.35	64.79	69.00	59.31
2.	Delhi	55.61	63.71	47.75	61.54	68.40	53.07
3.	Mizoram	53.79	60.49	46.71	59.88	64.46	54.51
4.	Pondicherry	46.02	57.29	44.62	55.85	65.84	45.71
5.	Goa, Daman & Diu	49.71	54.31	35.09	56.61	65.59	47.56
6.	Lakshadweep	43.66	56.48	30.56	55.07	65.24	44.65
7.	Dadra & Nagar Haveli	14.97	22.15	7.84	46.67	36.32	16.78
8.	A.& N. Islands	43.59	51.64	31.11	51.56	58.72	42.14
9.	Arunachal Pradesh	11.29	17.82	03.71	20.79	28.94	11.32
	INDIA	29.45	39.45	18.69	36.23	46.89	24.82

TWO Best Positions 1971 Chandigarh 61.56 Kerala 60.42
TWO Best Positions 1981 Kerala 70.74 Chandigarh 64.79.

5

STATE EDUCATION PROFILE

TABLE 5.1: **Andhra Pradesh: Populations 99,21,300**

Sl No.	*Type of Institution*	*No. of Institutions*		*No. of Inhabitants served by one Institution*
		Total No.	*No. per 10 lakh of Population*	
1.	Pre-Primary/Pre-Basic School	34	0.57	1,762,391
2.	Primary/Junior Basic School	44,299	739.10	1,353
3.	Middle/Senior Basic School	5,672	94.66	10,564
4.	High/Post-Basic School	4,909	81.93	12,206
5.	Higher Secondary Old Pattern School	—	—	—
6.	Higher Secondary (10+2) Institution	48	0.80	1,248,360
7.	Intermediate/Junior College	636	10.61	94,216
8.	Board of Intermediate/Secondary Education	2	0.03	29,960,650
9.	Teacher Training College	33	0.55	1,815,797
10.	Teacher Training School	23	0.38	2,605,274
11.	Polytechnic Institute	74	1.23	809,747
12.	Technical Industrial Arts/Crafts School	361	6.02	165,987
13.	Arts/Science/Commerce College	352	5.87	170,231
14.	Engineering & Technical College	27	0.45	2,219,307
15.	Medical College	9	0.15	6,657,922
16.	Universities	14	0.23	428,093

Sl. No.	*Category of Enrolment*	*No. of Students enrolled*		*No. of Inhabitants Per Student Enrolled*
		Total No.	*No. per 10,000 of Population*	
1.	Pre-Primary/Pre-Basic Stage	18,424	3.08	3,252
2.	Primary Stage (Class I-V)	6,924,592	1,111.11	9
3.	Middle/Senior Basic Stage (VI-VIII)	1,396,069	232.56	43
4.	High/Post-Basic Stage (IX-X)	1,355,326	227.27	44
5.	Higher Secondary Old Pattern	—	—	—
6.	Higher Secondary (10+2)	1,993	0.33	30,066
7.	Pre-University	—	—	—
8.	Pre-Degree/Pre-University	—	—	—
9.	Intermediate/Junior College	373,392	62.50	160
10.	B.A./B.A.(Hons.)	72,315	12.06	829
11.	B.Sc./B.Sc.(Hons.)	63,804	10.64	939
12.	B.Com./B.Com. (Hons.)	85,591	14.29	700
13.	M.A.	7,650	1.28	7,833
14.	M.Sc.	5,024	0.84	11,927
15.	M.Com.	5,028	0.84	11,918
16.	Ph.D.	1,664	0.28	36,010
17.	B.Ed./B.T.	4,820	0.80	12,432
18.	B.E./B.Sc.(Engg.)/B.Architect	16,130	2.69	3,715
19.	M.B.B.S.	6,761	1.13	8,863

TABLE 5.2: **Assam: Population: 2,28,21,100**

Sl. No.	Type of Institution	No. of Institutions		No. of Inhabitants served by one Institution
		Total No.	No per 10 lakh of population	
1.	Pre-Primary/Pre-Basic School	482	21.12	47,347
2.	Primary/Junior Basic School	25,970	1137.66	879
3.	Middle/Senior Basic School	5,356	234.69	4,261
4.	High/Post-Basic School	2,593	113.62	8,801
5.	Higher Secondary Old Pattern School	—	—	—
6.	Higher Secondary (10+2) Institution	356	15.60	64,104
7.	Intermediate/Junior College	5	0.22	45,64,220
8.	Board of Intermediate/Secondary Education	2	0.09	1,14,10,550
9.	Teacher Training College	8	0.35	28,52,638
10.	Teacher Training School	32	1.40	7,13,159
11.	Polytechnic Institute	6	0.26	38,03,517
12.	Technical Industrial Arts/Crafts School	27	1.18	8,45,226
13.	Arts/Science/Commerce College	160	7.01	1,42,632
14.	Engineering & Technical College	3	0.13	76,07,033
15.	Medical College	3	0.13	76,07,033
16.	Universities	3	0.13	76,07,033

Sl. No.	Category of Enrolment	No. of Students Enrolled		No. of Inhabitants per student enrolled
		Total No.	No. per 10,000 of Population	
1.	Pre-Primary/Pre-Basic Stage	20,218	8.86	1,129
2.	Primary Stage (Class I-V)	27,90,002	1,250.00	8
3.	Middle/Senior Basic Stage (VI-VIII)	11,51,744	500.00	20
4.	High/Post-Basic Stage (IX-X)	5,17,570	227.27	44
5.	Higher Secondary Old Pattern	—	—	—
6.	Higher Secondary (10+2)	1,36,615	59.88	167
7.	Pre-University	—	—	—
8.	Pre-Degree/Pre-University	—	—	—
9.	Intermediate/Junior College	—	—	—
10.	B.A./B.A. (Hons.)	43,929	19.27	519
11.	B.Sc./B.Sc. (Hons.)	11,669	5.11	1,956
12.	B.Com./B.Com. (Hons.)	6,697	2.93	3,408
13.	M.A.	2,540	1.11	8,985
14.	M.Sc.	1,286	0.56	17,746
15.	M.Com.	384	0.17	59,430
16.	Ph.D.	211	0.09	1,08,157
17.	B.Ed./B.T.	1,125	0.49	20,285
18.	B.E./B.Sc.(Engg.) B.Architect	2,592	1.14	8,804
19.	M.B.B.S.	1,902	0.83	11,998

TABLE 5.3: **Bihar: Population: 7,93,18,600**

Sl. No.	*Type of Institution*	*No. of Institutions*		*No. of Inhabitants served by one Institution*
		Total No.	*No. per 10 lakh of population*	
1.	Pre-Primary/Pre-Basic School	3	0.04	2,64,39,533
2.	Primary/Junior Basic School	50,920	641.85	1,558
3.	Middle/Senior Basic School	11,893	149.95	6,669
4.	High/Post Basic School	3,616	45.59	21,935
5.	Higher Secondary Old Pattern School	–	–	–
6.	Higher Secondary (10+2) Institution	167	2.11	4,74,962
7.	Intermediate/Junior College	3	0.04	26,439,533
8.	Board of Intermediate/Secondary Education	2	0.03	39,659,300
9.	Teacher Training College	15	0.19	52,87,907
10.	Teacher Training School	95	1.20	8,34,933
11.	Polytechnic Institute	16	0.20	49,57,413
12.	Technical Industrial Arts/Crafts School	30	0.38	26,43,953
13.	Arts/Science/Commerce College	342	4.31	2,31,926
14.	Engineering & Technical College	6	0.08	13,219,767
15.	Medical College	10	0.13	7,931,860
16.	Universities	10	0.13	7,931,860

Sl. No.	*Category of Enrolment*	*No. of Students enrolled*		*No. of Inhabitants per student enrolled*
		Total No.	*No. per 10,000 of Population*	
1.	Pre-Primary/Pre-Basic Stage	28,340	3.57	2,799
2.	Primary Stage (Class I-V)	80,30,064	1000.00	10
3.	Middle/Senior Basic Stage (VI-VIII)	18,73,304	238.10	42
4.	High/Post Basic Stage (IX-X)	7,50,366	94.34	106
5.	Higher Secondary Old Pattern	–	–	–
6.	Higher Secondary (10+2)	15,793	1.99	5,022
7.	Pre-University	–	–	–
8.	Pre-Degree/Pre-University	–	–	–
9.	Intermediate/Junior College	3,21,598	40.49	247
10.	B.A./B.A.(Hons.)	1,16,623	14.71	680
11.	B.Sc./B.Sc.(Hons.)	56,620	7.14	1,401
12.	B.Com./B.Com. (Hons.)	28,623	3.61	2,771
13.	M.A.	10,025	1.26	7,912
14.	M.Sc.	2,818	0.36	28,147
15.	M.Com.	792	0.10	1,00,150
16.	Ph.D.	379	0.05	2,09,284
17.	B.Ed./B.T.	6,205	0.78	12,783
18.	B.E./B.Sc.(Engg.)/B.Architect	6,697	0.84	11,844
19.	M.B.B.S.	4,398	0.55	18,035

TABLE 5.4: **Gujarat: Population: 3,84,28,000**

Sl. No.	*Type of Institution*	*No. of Institutions*		*No. of Inhabitants served by one Institution*
		Total No.	*No. per 10 lakh of population*	
1.	Pre-Primary/Pre-Basic School	1,900	49.44	20,225
2.	Primary/Junior Basic School	11,950	310.95	3,216
3.	Middle/Senior Basic School	15,450	402.09	2,487
4.	High/Post-Basic School	3,180	82.75	12,084
5.	Higher Secondary Old Pattern School	—	—	—
6.	Higher Secondary (10+2) Institution	1,276	33.20	30,116
7.	Intermediate/Junior College	—	—	—
8.	Board of Intermediate/Secondary Education	1	0.03	3,84,28,000
9.	Teacher Training College	38	0.99	10,11,263
10.	Teacher Training School	88	2.29	4,36,682
11.	Polytechnic Institute	19	0.49	20,22,526
12.	Technical Industrial Arts/Crafts School	675	17.57	56,930
13.	Arts/Science/Commerce College	211	5.49	1,82,123
14.	Engineering & Technical College	10	0.26	38,42,800
15.	Medical College	5	0.13	76,85,600
16.	Universities	10	0.26	38,42,800

Sl. No.	*Category of Enrolment*	*No. of Students enrolled*		*No. of Inhabitants per student enrolled*
		Total No.	*No. per 10,000 of Population*	
1.	Pre-Primary/Pre-Basic Stage	1,30,000	33.78	296
2.	Primary Stage (Class I-V)	50,68,000	1250.00	8
3.	Middle/Senior Basic Stage (VI-VIII)	13,98,000	370.37	27
4.	High/Post-Basic Stage (IX-X)	6,13,000	158.73	63
5.	Higher Secondary Old Pattern	—	—	—
6.	Higher Secondary (10+2)	2,76,000	71.94	139
7.	Pre-University	—	—	—
8.	Pre-Degree/Pre-University	-	-	-
9.	Intermediate/Junior College	-	-	-
10.	B.A./B.A. (Hons.)	63,600	16.56	604
11.	B.Sc./B.Sc. (Hons.)	24,700	6.42	15,558
12.	B.Com./B.Com. (Hons.)	77,100	20.08	498
13.	M.A.	4,000	1.04	9,607
14.	M.Sc.	2,850	0.74	13,484
15.	M.Com.	3,800	0.99	10,113
16.	Ph.D.	1,200	0.31	32,023
17.	B.Ed./B.T.	5,000	1.30	7,686
18.	B.E./B.Sc.(Engg.)/B.Architect	12,000	3.12	3,202
19.	M.B.B.S.	5,900	1.54	6,513

TABLE 5.5: **Haryana: Population 1,51,97,400**

Sl. No.	Type of Institution	No. of Institutions		No. of Inhabitants served by one Institution
		Total No.	No. per 10 lakh of population	
1.	Pre-Primary/Pre-Basic School	27	1.78	5,62,867
2.	Primary/Junior Basic School	5,131	337.61	2,962
3.	Middle/Senior Basic School	1,139	74.95	13,343
4.	High/Post-Basic School	1,893	124.56	8,028
5.	Higher Secondary Old Pattern School	—	—	—
6.	Higher Secondary (10+2) Institution	174	11.45	87,341
7.	Intermediate/Junior College	—	—	—
8.	Board of Intermediate/Secondary Education	1	0.07	1,51,97,400
9.	Teacher Training College	18	1.18	8,44,300
10.	Teacher Training School	—	—	—
11.	Polytechnic Institute	20	1.32	7,59,870
12.	Technical Industrial Arts/Crafts School	110	7.24	1,38,158
13.	Arts/Science/Commerce College	110	7.24	1,38,158
14.	Engineering & Technical College	2	0.13	75,98,700
15.	Medical College	1	0.07	1,51,97,400
16.	Universities	4	0.26	37,99,350

Sl. No.	Category of Enrolment	No. of Students enrolled		No. of Inhabitants per student enrolled
		Total No.	No. per 10,000 of Population	
1.	Pre-Primary/Pre-Basic Stage	5,929	3.90	2,563
2.	Primary Stage (Class I-V)	15,99,406	1,000.00	10
3.	Middle/Senior Basic Stage (VI-VIII)	6,43,190	416.67	24
4.	High/Post Basic Stage (IX-X)	2,23,460	147.06	68
5.	Higher Secondary Old Pattern	33,192	21.83	458
6.	Higher Secondary (10+2)	NA	—	—
7.	Pre-University	—	—	—
8.	Pre-Degree/Pre-University	—	—	—
9.	Intermediate/Junior College	63,292	41.67	240
10.	B.A./B.A. (Hons.)	28,299	18.62	537
11.	B.Sc./B.Sc. (Hons.)	6,229	4.10	2,440
12.	B.Com./B.Com. (Hons.)	6,830	4.49	2,225
13.	M.A.	3,731	2.46	4,073
14.	M.Sc.	591	0.39	25,715
15.	M.Com.	243	0.16	62,541
16.	Ph.D.	643	0.42	23,635
17.	B.Ed./B.T.	3,448	2.27	4,408
18.	B.E./B.Sc.(Engg.)/B.Architect	1,502	0.99	10,118
19.	M.B.B.S.	610	0.40	24,914

TABLE 5.6: **Himachal Pradesh: Population 47,87,300**

Sl. No.	*Type of Institution*	*No. of Institutions*		*No. of Inhabitants served by one Institution*
		Total No.	*No. per 10 lakh of population*	
1.	Pre-Primary/Pre-Basic School	10	2.08	4,78,700
2.	Primary/Junior Basic School	6,864	1,428.57	700
3.	Middle/Senior Basic School	1,025	212.76	4,700
4.	High/Post-Basic School	699	147.05	6,800
5.	Higher Secondary Old Pattern School	—	—	—
6.	Higher Secondary (10+2) Institution	101	21.09	47,400
7.	Intermediate/Junior College	—	—	—
8.	Board of Intermediate/Secondary Education	1	0.20	47,87,300
9.	Teacher Training College	2	0.41	23,93,700
10.	Teacher Training School	6	1.25	7,97,900
11.	Polytechnic Institute	4	0.83	11,96,825
12.	Technical Industrial Arts/Crafts School	32	6.68	1,49,600
13.	Arts/Science/Commerce College	37	7.72	1,29,400
14.	Engineering & Technical College	1	0.20	47,87,300
15.	Medical College	1	0.20	47,87,300
16.	Universities	3	0.62	15,95,800

Sl. No.	*Category of Enrolment*	*No. of Students enrolled*		*No. of Inhabitants per student enrolled*
		Total No.	*No. per 10,000 of Population*	
1.	Pre-Primary/Pre-Basic Stage	6,249	13.50	7,660
2.	Primary Stage (Class I-V)	6,44,482	1347.70	7.42
3.	Middle/Senior Basic Stage (VI-VIII)	3,01,571	630.12	15.87
4.	High/Post-Basic Stage (IX-X)	1,00,895	210.74	47.45
5.	Higher Secondary Old Pattern	9,683	20.22	494.40
6.	Higher Secondary (10+2)	18,764	39.19	255.13
7.	Pre-University	11,868	24.79	403.38
8.	Pre-Degree/Pre-University	-	-	
9.	Intermediate/Junior College	-	-	-
10.	B.A./B.A.(Hons.)	13,704	28.65	349.33
11.	B.Sc./B.Sc.(Hons.)	2,930	6.12	1,633.89
12.	B.Com./B.Com. (Hons.)	1,134	2.36	4,221.60
13.	M.A.	805	1.68	5,946.95
14.	M.Sc.	229	0.48	20,905.20
15.	M.Com.	87	0.18	55,024.43
16.	Ph.D.	860	1.79	5,566.62
17.	B.Ed./B.T.	146	0.30	32,789.72
18.	B.E./B.Sc.(Engg.)/B.Architect		-	
19.	M.B.B.S.	373	0.77	12,834.58

TABLE 5.7: **Jammu & Kashmir: Population: 68,45,600**

Sl. No.	*Type of Institution*	*No. of Institutions*		*No. of Inhabitants served by one Institution*
		Total No.	*No. per 10 lakh of population*	
1.	Pre-Primary/Pre-Basic School	—	—	—
2.	Primary/Junior Basic School	8,106	1,183.43	845
3.	Middle/Senior Basic School	2,288	334.22	2,992
4.	High/Post-Basic School	849	124.02	8,063
5.	Higher Secondary Old Pattern School	—	—	—
6.	Higher Secondary (10+2) Institution	179	26.15	38,244
7.	Intermediate/Junior College	—	—	—
8.	Board of Intermediate/Secondary Education	1	0.15	68,45,600
9.	Teacher Training College.	3	0.44	22,81,867
10.	Teacher Training School	14	2.05	4,88,971
11.	Polytechnic Institute	2	0.29	34,22,800
12.	Technical Industrial Arts/Crafts School	20	2.92	3,42,280
13.	Arts/Science/Commerce College	26	3.80	2,63,292
14.	Engineering & Technical College	1	0.15	68,45,600
15.	Medical College	2	0.29	34,22,800
16.	Universities	2	0.29	34,22,800

Sl. No.	*Category of Enrolment*	*No. of Students enrolled*		*No. of Inhabitants per student enrolled*
		Total No.	*No. per 10,000 of Population*	
1.	Pre-Primary/Pre-Basic Stage	12,180	17.79	562
2.	Primary Stage (Class I-V)	6,67,000	1000.00	10
3.	Middle/Senior Basic Stage (VI-VIII)	2,45,000	357.14	28
4.	High/Post-Basic Stage (IX-X)	86,000	125.00	80
5.	Higher Secondary Old Pattern			
6.	Higher Secondary (10+2)	42,000	61.35	163
7.	Pre-University	800	1.17	8,557
8.	Pre-Degree/Pre-University			
9.	Intermediate/Junior College			
10.	B.A./B.A.(Hons.)	9,330	13.62	734
11.	B.Sc./B.Sc.(Hons.)	7,520	10.99	910
12.	B.Com./B.Com. (Hons.)	1,380	2.02	4,961
13.	M.A.	1,520	2.22	4,504
14.	M.Sc.	738	1.08	9,276
15.	M.Com.	207	0.30	33,070.5
16.	Ph.D.	364	0.53	18,807
17.	B.Ed./B.T.	960	1.40	7,131
18.	B.E./B.Sc.(Engg.)/B.Architect	1,880	2.75	3,641
19.	M.B.B.S.	1,220	1.78	5,611

TABLE 5.8: **Karnataka: Population: 4,21,70,500**

Sl. No.	Type of Institution	No. of Institutions		No. of Inhabitants served by one Institution
		Total No.	No. per 10 lakh of population	
1.	Pre-Primary/Pre-Basic School	5,184	122.93	8,135
2.	Primary/Junior Basic School	24,735	586.51	1,705
3.	Middle/Senior Basic School	14,120	334.78	2,987
4.	High/Post-Basic School	3,805	90.23	11,083
5.	Higher Secondary Old Pattern School	—	—	—
6.	Higher Secondary (10+2) Institution	871	20.65	48,416
7.	Intermediate/Junior College	189	4.48	2,23,124
8.	Board of Intermediate/Secondary Education	2	0.05	2,10,85,250
9.	Teacher Training College	58	1.38	7,27,078
10.	Teacher Training School	165	3.91	2,55,579
11.	Polytechnic Institute	163	3.87	2,58,715
12.	Technical Industrial Arts/Crafts School	117	2.77	3,60,432
13.	Arts/Science/Commerce College	367	8.70	1,14,906
14.	Engineering & Technical College	50	1.19	8,43,410
15.	Medical College	12	0.28	35,14,208
16.	Universities	7	0.17	60,24,357

Sl. No.	Category of Enrolment	No. of Students enrolled		No. of Inhabitants per student enrolled
		Total No.	No. per 10,000 of Population	
1.	Pre-Primary/Pre-Basic Stage	3,12,730	74.07	135
2.	Primary Stage (Class I-V)	48,35,006	1111.11	9
3.	Middle/Senior Basic Stage (VI-VIII)	20,33,135	476.19	21
4.	High/Post-Basic Stage (IX-X)	7,63,564	181.20	55.2
5.	Higher Secondary Old Pattern	—	—	—
6.	Higher Secondary (10+2)	1,56,286	37.04	270
7.	Pre-University		—	—
8.	Pre-Degree/Pre-University		—	—
9.	Intermediate/Junior College	38,914	9.23	1,084
10.	B.A./B.A.(Hons.)	1,15,344	27.32	366
11.	B.Sc./B.Sc.(Hons.)	44,953	10.66	938
12.	B.Com./B.Com. (Hons.)	66,153	15.70	637
13.	M.A.	10,191	2.42	4,138
14.	M.Sc.	10,271	2.44	4,106
15.	M.Com.	977	0.23	43,163
16.	Ph.D.	537	0.13	78,530
17.	B.Ed./B.T.	4,511	1.07	9,348
18.	B.E./B.Sc.(Engg.)/B.Architect	40,498	9.61	1,041
19.	M.B.B.S.	7,360	1.75	5,730

TABLE 5.9: **Kerala: Population: 2,83,30,900**

Sl. No.	*Type of Institution*	*No. of Institutions*		*No. of Inhabitants served by one Institution*
		Total No.	*No. per 10 lakh of population*	
1.	Pre-Primary/Pre-Basic School	206	7.27	1,37,529
2.	Primary/Junior Basic School	6,828	241.02	4,149
3.	Middle/Senior Basic School	2,884	101.80	9,823
4.	High/Post-Basic School	2,430	85.77	11,659
5.	Higher Secondary Old Pattern School	—	—	—
6.	Higher Secondary (10+2) Institution	37	1.31	7,65,700
7.	Intermediate/Junior College	43	1.52	6,58,858
8.	Board of Intermediate/Secondary Education	1	0.04	2,83,30,900
9.	Teacher Training College	19	0.67	14,91,100
10.	Teacher Training School	94	3.32	3,01,393
11.	Polytechnic Institute	25	0.88	11,33,236
12.	Technical Industrial Arts/Crafts School	151	5.33	1,87,622
13.	Arts/Science/Commerce College	142	5.01	1,99,513
14.	Engineering & Technical College	7	0.25	40,47,271
15.	Medical College	5	0.18	56,66,180
16.	Universities	6	0.21	47,21,817

Sl. No.	*Category of Enrolment*	*No. of Students enrolled*		*No. of Inhabitants per student enrolled*
		Total No.	*No. per 10,000 of Population*	
1.	Pre-Primary/Pre-Basic Stage	13,416	4.73	2,112
2.	Primary Stage (Class 1-V)	32,10,857	1,111.11	9
3.	Middle/Senior Basic Stage (VI-VIII)	16,96,673	588.24	17
4.	High/Post Basic Stage (IX-X)	8,09,927	285.71	35
5.	Higher Secondary Old Pattern	—	—	—
6.	Higher Secondary (10+2)	1,067	0.38	26,552
7.	Pre-University	—	—	—
8.	Pre-Degree/Pre-University	2,13,404	75.19	133
9.	Intermediate/Junior College	—	—	—
10.	B.A./B.A. (Hons.)	4,6356	16.37	611
11.	B.Sc./B.Sc. (Hons.)	49,688	17.54	570
12.	B.Com./B.Com. (Hons.)	18,404	6.50	1,539
13.	M.A.	4,570	1.61	6,199
14.	M.Sc.	4,296	1.52	6,595
15.	M.Com.	1,444	0.51	19,620
16.	Ph.D.	1,144	0.40	24,765
17.	B.Ed./B.T.	3,778	1.33	7,499
18.	B.E./B.Sc.(Engg.) B.Architect	11,001	3.88	2,575
19.	M.B.B.S.	5,223	1.84	5,424

TABLE 5.10: **Madhya Pradesh: Population: 5,93,88,400**

Sl. No.	*Type of Institution*	*No. of Institutions*		*No. of Inhabitants served by one Institution*
		Total No.	*No. per 10 lakh of population*	
1.	Pre-Primary/Pre-Basic School	684	11.52	86,825
2.	Primary/Junior Basic School	65,147	1,096.49	912
3.	Middle/Senior Basic School	13,253	223.16	4,481
4.	High/Post-Basic School	1,430	24.08	41,530
5.	Higher Secondary Old Pattern School	—	—	—
6.	Higher Secondary (10+2) Institution	1,752	29.50	33897
7.	Intermediate/Junior College	—	—	—
8.	Board of Intermediate/Secondary Education	1	0.02	5,93,88,400
9.	Teacher Training College	19	0.32	31,25,705
10.	Teacher Training School	49	0.83	12,12,008
11.	Polytechnic Institute	14	0.24	42,42,029
12.	Technical Industrial Arts/Crafts School	58	0.98	10,23,938
13.	Arts/Science/Commerce College	360	6.06	1,64,968
14.	Engineering & Technical College	10	0.17	59,38,840
15.	Medical College	6	0.10	98,98,067
16.	Universities	11	0.19	53,98,945

Sl. No.	*Category of Enrolment*	*No. of Students enrolled*		*No. of Inhabitants per student enrolled*
		Total No.	*No. per 10,000 of Population*	
1.	Pre-Primary/Pre-Basic Stage	85,815	14.45	692
2.	Primary Stage (Class I-V)	70,90,432	1,250.00	8
3.	Middle/Senior Basic Stage (VI-VIII)	19,55,980	333.33	30
4.	High/Post-Basic Stage (IX-X)	3,12,588	52.63	190
5.	Higher Secondary Old Pattern	—	—	—
6.	Higher Secondary (10+2)	5,74,221	97.09	103
7.	Pre-University	—	—	—
8.	Pre-Degree/Pre-University	—	—	—
9.	Intermediate/Junior College	—	—	—
10.	B.A./B.A. (Hons.)	92,932	15.65	639
11.	B.Sc./B.Sc. (Hons.)	51,237	8.63	1,159
12.	B.Com./B.Com. (Hons.)	49,849	8.40	1,191
13.	M.A.	15,173	2.55	3,914
14.	M.Sc.	7,798	1.31	7,616
15.	M.Com.	8,051	1.36	7,377
16.	Ph.D.	2,111	0.36	28,133
17.	B.Ed./B.T.	4,497	0.76	13,206
18.	B.E./B.Sc.(Engg.)/B.Architect	2,278	0.38	26,070
19.	M.B.B.S.	4,224	0.71	14,060

TABLE 5.11: **Maharashtra: Population: 7,11,21,700**

Sl. No.	*Type of Institution*	*No. of Institutions*		*No. of Inhabitants served by one Institution*
		Total No.	*No. per 10 lakh of population*	
1.	Pre-Primary/Pre-Basic School	725	10.19	98,099
2.	Primary/Junior Basic School	36,500	541.42	1,847
3.	Middle/Senior Basic School	16,800	236.24	4,233
4.	High/Post-Basic School	6,975	98.07	10,197
5.	Higher Secondary Old Pattern School	—	—	—
6.	Higher Secondary (10+2) Institution	1,225	17.22	58,059
7.	Intermediate/Junior College	—	—	—
8.	Board of Intermediate/Secondary Education	1	0.01	7,11,21,700
9.	Teacher Training College	77	1.08	9,23,658
10.	Teacher Training School	6	0.08	1,18,53,617
11.	Polytechnic Institute	140	1.97	5,08,012
12.	Technical Industrial Arts/Crafts School	1,200	16.87	59,268
13.	Arts/Science/Commerce College	520	7.31	1,36,773
14.	Engineering & Technical College	69	0.97	10,30,749
15.	Medical College	16	0.22	44,45,106
16.	Universities	13	0.18	54,70,900

Sl. No.	*Category of Enrolment*	*No. of Students enrolled*		*No. of Inhabitants per student enrolled*
		Total No.	*No. per 10,000 of Population*	
1.	Pre-Primary/Pre-Basic Stage	1,40,000	19.69	508
2.	Primary Stage (Class I-V)	94,65,000	1250.00	8
3.	Middle/Senior Basic Stage (VI-VIII).	32,28,000	454.55	22
4.	High/Post-Basic Stage (IX-X)	14,23,000	200.00	50
5.	Higher Secondary Old Pattern	—	—	—
6.	Higher Secondary (10+2)	6,35,000	89.29	112
7.	Pre-University	—	—	—
8.	Pre-Degree/Pre-University	—	—	—
9.	Intermediate/Junior College	—	—	—
10.	B.A./B.A.(Hons.)	1,02,500	14.41	694
11.	B.Sc./B.Sc.(Hons.)	60,000	8.44	1,185
12.	B.Com./B.Com. (Hons.)	1,79,500	25.25	396
13.	M.A.	14,700	2.07	4,838
14.	M.Sc.	6,600	0.93	10,776
15.	M.Com.	15,700	2.21	4,530
16.	Ph.D.	3,850	0.54	18,473
17.	B.Ed./B.T.	10,650	1.50	6,678
18.	B.E./B.Sc. (Engg.)/B.Architect	30,600	4.30	2,324
19.	M.B.B.S.	9,500	1.34	7,486

TABLE 5.12: **Manipur: Population: 16,48,900**

Sl. No.	Type of Institution	No. of Institutions: Total No.	No. of Institutions: No. per 10 lakh of population	No. of Inhabitants served by one Institution
1.	Pre-Primary/Pre-Basic School	1	0.61	16,48,900
2.	Primary/Junior Basic School	2,678	1,623.38	616
3.	Middle/Senior Basic School	440	266.81	3,748
4.	High/Post-Basic School	348	211.06	4,738
5.	Higher Secondary Old Pattern School	—	—	—
6.	Higher Secondary (10+2) Institution	10	6.06	1,64,890
7.	Intermediate/Junior College	5	3.03	3,29,780
8.	Board of Intermediate/Secondary Education	1	0.61	16,48,900
9.	Teacher Training College	3	1.82	5,49,633
10.	Teacher Training School	3	1.82	5,49,633
11.	Polytechnic Institute	1	0.61	16,43,900
12.	Technical Industrial Arts/Crafts School	25	12.74	78,519
13.	Arts/Science/Commerce College	23	13.95	71,691
14.	Engineering & Technical College	—	—	—
15.	Medical College	1	0.61	16,48,900
16.	Universities	1	0.61	16,48,900

Sl. No.	Category of Enrolment	No. of Students enrolled: Total No.	No. of Students enrolled: No. per 10,000 of Population	No. of Inhabitants per student enrolled
1.	Pre-Primary/Pre-Basic Stage	380	2.30	4,339
2.	Primary Stage (Class I-V)	2,39,150	1,428.57	7
3.	Middle/Senior Basic Stage (VI-VIII)	78,750	476.19	21
4.	High/Post-Basic Stage (IX-X)	45,320	277.78	36
5.	Higher Secondary Old Pattern	—	—	—
6.	Higher Secondary (10+2)	1,160	7.04	1,421
7.	Pre-University	—	—	—
8.	Pre-Degree/Pre-University	16,030	97.09	103
9.	Intermediate/Junior College	1,750	10.62	942
10.	B.A./B.A. (Hons.)	7,260	44.05	227
11.	B.Sc./B.Sc. (Hons.)	2,740	16.61	602
12.	B.Com./B.Com. (Hons.)	230	1.39	7,169
13.	M.A.	830	5.03	1,987
14.	M.Sc.	310	1.88	5,319
15.	M.Com.	20	0.12	82,445
16.	Ph.D.	220	1.33	7,495
17.	B.Ed./B.T.		—	
18.	B.E./B.Sc.(Engg.) B.Architect	—	—	—
19.	M.B.B.S.	460	2.79	3,585

TABLE 5.13: **Meghalaya:Population: 15,74,900**

Sl. No.	Type of Institution	No. of Institutions		No. of Inhabitants served by one Institution
		Total No.	No. per 10 lakh of population	
1.	Pre-Primary/Pre-Basic School	1,005	638.16	1,567
2.	Primary/Junior Basic School	4,155	2,638.52	379
3.	Middle/Senior Basic School	615	390.47	2,561
4.	High/Post-Basic School	281	178.41	5,605
5.	Higher Secondary Old Pattern School	—	—	—
6.	Higher Secondary (10+2) Institution	—	—	—
7.	Intermediate/Junior College	—	—	—
8.	Board of Intermediate/Secondary Education	1	0.63	15,74,900
9.	Teacher Training College	1	0.63	15,74,900
10.	Teacher Training School	10	6.35	1,57,490
11.	Polytechnic Institute	1	0.63	15,74,900
12.	Technical Industrial Arts/Crafts School	30	19.05	52,497
13.	Arts/Science/Commerce College	14	8.89	1,12,493
14.	Engineering & Technical College	—	—	—
15.	Medical College	—	—	—
16.	Universities	1	0.63	15,74,900

Sl. No.	Category of Enrolment	No. of Students enrolled		No. of Inhabitants per student enrolled
		Total No.	No. per 10,000 of Population	
1.	Pre-Primary/Pre-Basic Stage	50,642	322.58	31
2.	Primary Stage (Class I-V)	207,923	1,250.00	8
3.	Middle/Senior Basic Stage (VI-VIII)	63,905	400.00	25
4.	High/Post-Basic Stage (IX-X)	39,388	250.00	40
5.	Higher Secondary Old Pattern	—	—	—
6.	Higher Secondary (10+2)	—	—	—
7.	Pre-University	—	—	—
8.	Pre-Degree/Pre-University	10,245	64.94	154
9.	Intermediate/Junior College	—	—	—
10.	B.A./B.A. (Hons.)	3,776	23.98	417
11.	B.Sc./B.Sc. (Hons.)	1,108	7.04	1,421
12.	B.Com./B.Com. (Hons.)	438	2.78	3,596
13.	M.A.	345	3.46	2,890
14.	M.Sc.	128	0.81	12,304
15.	M.Com.	17	0.11	92,641
16.	Ph.D.	63	0.40	24,998
17.	B.Ed./B.T.	452	2.87	3,484
18.	B.E./B.Sc.(Engg.)/B.Architect	—	—	—
19.	M.B.B.S.	—	—	—

TABLE 5.14: **Nagaland: Population: 9,82,200**

Sl. No.	*Type of Institution*	*No. of Institutions*		*No. of Inhabitants served by one Institution*
		Total No.	*No. per 10 lakh of population*	
1.	Pre-Primary/Pre-Basic School	—	—	—
2.	Primary/Junior Basic School	1,270	1,293.66	773
3.	Middle/Senior Basic School	343	349.16	2,864
4.	High/Post-Basic School	3	3.05	3,27,400
5.	Higher Secondary Old Pattern School	—	—	—
6.	Higher Secondary (10+2) Institution	—	—	—
7.	Intermediate/Junior College	—	—	—
8.	Board of Intermediate/Secondary Education	1	1.02	9,82,200
9.	Teacher Training College	1	1.02	9,82,200
10.	Teacher Training School	3	3.05	3,27,400
11.	Polytechnic Institute	1	1.02	9,82,200
12.	Technical Industrial Arts/Crafts School	1	1,02	9,82,200
13.	Arts/Science/Commerce College	15	15.27	65,480
14.	Engineering & Technical College	1	1.02	9,82,200
15.	Medical College	—	—	—
16.	Universities	—	—	—

Sl. No.	*Category of Enrolment*	*No. of Students enrolled*		*No. of Inhabitants per student enrolled*
		Total No.	*No. per 10,000 of Population*	
1.	Pre-Primary/Pre-Basic Stage	73,400	769.23	13
2.	Primary Stage (Class I-V)	1,40,232	1,428.57	7
3.	Middle/Senior Basic Stage (VI-VIII)	36,300	3,70.1	27
4.	High/Post-Basic Stage (IX-X)	15,500	158.73	63
5.	Higher Secondary Old Pattern	—	—	—
6.	Higher Secondary (10+2)	—	—	—
7.	Pre-University	—	—	—
8.	Pre-Degree/Pre-University	4623	47.17	212
9.	Intermediate/Junior College	—	—	—
10.	B.A./B.A. (Hons.)	1,442	14.68	681
11.	B.Sc./B.Sc. (Hons.)	286	2.91	3,434
12.	B.Com./B.Com. (Hons.)	127	1.29	7,734
13.	M.A.	—	—	—
14.	M.Sc.	5	0.05	1,96,440
15.	M.Com.	—	—	—
16.	Ph.D.	—	—	—
17.	B.Ed./B.T.	67	0.68	14,660
18.	B.E./B.Sc.(Engg.)/B.Architect	—	—	—
19.	M.B.B.S.			

TABLE 5.15: **Orissa: Population: 2,93,59,000**

Sl. No.	Type of Institution	No. of Institutions: Total No.	No. of Institutions: No. per 10 lakh of population	No. of Inhabitants served by one Institution
1.	Pre-Primary/Pre-Basic School	—	—	—
2.	Primary/Junior Basic School	37,993	1,293.66	773
3.	Middle/Senior Basic School	8,441	287.52	3,478
4.	High/Post-Basic School	3924	133.65	7,482
5.	Higher Secondary Old Pattern School	—	—	—
6.	Higher Secondary (10+2) Institution	—	—	—
7.	Intermediate/Junior College	173	5.89	1,69,705
8.	Board of Intermediate/Secondary Education	2	0.07	1,46,79,500
9.	Teacher Training College	34	1.16	8,63,500
10.	Teacher Training School	71	2.42	4,13,507
11.	Polytechnic Institute	4	0.14	73,39,750
12.	Technical Industrial Arts/Crafts School	19	0.65	15,45,211
13.	Arts/Science/Commerce College	154	5.25	1,90,643
14.	Engineering & Technical College	3	0.10	97,86,333
15.	Medical College	3	0.10	97,86,333
16.	Universities	5	0.17	58,71,800

Sl. No.	Category of Enrolment	No. of Students enrolled: Total No.	No. of Students enrolled: No. per 10,000 of Population	No. of Inhabitants per student enrolled
1.	Pre-Primary/Pre-Basic Stage	—	—	—
2.	Primary Stage (Class I-V)	33,26,000	1,111.11	9
3.	Middle/Senior Basic Stage (VI-VIII)	8,02,000	270.27	37
4.	High/Post-Basic Stage (IX-X)	4,41,911	151.52	66
5.	Higher Secondary Old Pattern	—	—	—
6.	Higher Secondary (10+2)	—	—	—
7.	Pre-University	—	—	—
8.	Pre-Degree/Pre-University	—	—	—
9.	Intermediate/Junior College	1,11,973	38.17	262
10.	B.A./B.A.(Hons.)	28,290	9.63	1,038
11.	B.Sc./B.Sc.(Hons.)	9,246	3.15	3,175
12.	B.Com./B.Com. (Hons.)	4,744	1.62	6,189
13.	M.A.	4,314	1.47	6,806
14.	M.Sc.	1,995	0.68	14,716
15.	M.Com.	662	0.23	44,349
16.	Ph.D.	206	0.07	1,42,519
17.	B.Ed./B.T.	2,240	0.76	13,107
18.	B.E./B.Sc.(Engg.)/B.Architect	2,154	0.73	13,630
19.	M.B.B.S.	1,712	0.58	17,149

TABLE 5.16: **Punjab: Population: 1,88,71,700**

Sl. No.	Type of Institution	No. of Institutions: Total No.	No. of Institutions: No. per 10 lakh of population	No. of Inhabitants served by one Institution
1.	Pre-Primary/Pre-Basic School	2	0.11	94,35,850
2.	Primary/Junior Basic School	12,322	652.74	1,532
3.	Middle/Senior Basic School	1,444	76.52	13,069
4.	High/Post-Basic School	2272	120.39	8,306
5.	Higher Secondary Old Pattern School	—	—	—
6.	Higher Secondary (10+2) Institution	280	14.84	67,399
7.	Intermediate/Junior College	—	—	—
8.	Board of Intermediate/Secondary Education	1	0.05	1,88,71,700
9.	Teacher Training College	18	0.95	10,48,428
10.	Teacher Training School	9	0.48	20,96,856
11.	Polytechnic Institute	10	0.53	18,87,170
12.	Technical Industrial Arts/Crafts School	97	5.14	1,94,554
13.	Arts/Science/Commerce College	169	8.96	1,11,667
14.	Engineering & Technical College	3	0.16	62,90,567
15.	Medical College	5	0.26	37,74,340
16.	Universities	3	0.16	62,90,567

Sl. No.	Category of Enrolment	No. of Students enrolled: Total No.	No. of Students enrolled: No. per 10,000 of Population	No. of Inhabitants per student enrolled
1.	Pre-Primary/Pre-Basic Stage	10,775	5.71	1,751
2.	Primary Stage (Class I-V)	19,96,597	1,111.11	9
3.	Middle/Senior Basic Stage (VI-VIII)	7,54,563	400.00	25
4.	High/Post-Basic Stage (IX-X)	2,45,514	129.87	77
5.	Higher Secondary Old Pattern	—	—	—
6.	Higher Secondary (10+2)	1,05,596	55.87	179
7.	Pre-University	39,326	20.83	480
8.	Pre-Degree/Pre-University	—	—	—
9.	Intermediate/Junior College	—	—	—
10.	B.A./B.A. (Hons.)	79,310	42.02	238
11.	B.Sc./B.Sc. (Hons.)	16,077	8.52	1,174
12.	B.Com./B.Com. (Hons.)	9,496	5.03	1,987
13.	M.A.	6,775	3.59	2,785
14.	M.Sc.	1,099	0.58	17,172
15.	M.Com.	137	0.07	1,37,750
16.	Ph.D.	585	0.31	32,259
17.	B.Ed./B.T.	3,069	1.63	6,149
18.	B.E./B.Sc.(Engg.)/B.Architect	1,762	0.93	10,710
19.	M.B.B.S.	2,362	1.25	7,990

TABLE 5.17: **Rajasthan: Population: 4,01,84,600**

Sl. No.	Type of Institution	No. of Institutions: Total No.	No. of Institutions: No. per 10 lakh of population	No. of Inhabitants served by one Institution
1.	Pre-Primary/Pre-Basic School	32	0.80	12,55,769
2.	Primary/Junior Basic School	28,139	700.28	1,428
3.	Middle/Senior Basic School	8,149	202.80	4,931
4.	High/Post-Basic School	2,166	53.90	18,552
5.	Higher Secondary Old Pattern School	892	22.20	45,050
6.	Higher Secondary (10+2) Institution	—	—	—
7.	Intermediate/Junior College	—	—	—
8.	Board of Intermediate/Secondary Education	2	0.05	2,00,92,300
9.	Teacher Training College	33	0.82	12,17,715
10.	Teacher Training School	34	0.85	11,81,900
11.	Polytechnic Institute	14	0.35	28,70,329
12.	Technical Industrial Arts/Crafts School	53	1.32	7,58,200
13.	Arts/Science/Commerce College	138	3.43	2,91,193
14.	Engineering & Technical College	3	0.07	1,33,94,867
15.	Medical College	5	0.12	80,36,920
16.	Universities	5	0.12	80,36,920

Sl. No.	Category of Enrolment	No. of Students enrolled: Total No.	No. of Students enrolled: No. per 10,000 of Population	No. of Inhabitants per student enrolled
1.	Pre-Primary/Pre-Basic Stage	1,02,902	25.58	391
2.	Primary Stage (Class I-V)	41,51,429	1,000.00	10
3.	Middle/Senior Basic Stage (VI-VIII)	11,58,662	285.71	35
4.	High/Post-Basic Stage (IX-X)	4,99,362	125.00	80
5.	Higher Secondary Old Pattern	1,17,307	29.15	343
6.	Higher Secondary (10+2)	—	—	—
7.	Pre-University	—	—	—
8.	Pre-Degree/Pre-University	—	—	—
9.	Intermediate/Junior College	—	—	—
10.	B.A./B.A. (Hons.)	48,148	11.98	835
11.	B.Sc./B.Sc. (Hons.)	28,758	7.16	1,397
12.	B.Com./B.Com. (Hons.)	52,597	13.09	764
13.	M.A.	15,354	3.82	2,617
14.	M.Sc.	2,711	0.67	14,823
15.	M.Com.	9,143	2.28	4,395
16.	Ph.D.	1,137	0.28	35,343
17.	B.Ed./B.T.	6,031	1.50	6,663
18.	B.E./B.Sc.(Engg.)/B.Architect	4,551	1.13	8,830
19.	M.B.B.S.	4,017	1.00	10,004

TABLE 5.18: **Sikkim: Population: 3,93,200**

Sl. No.	Type of Institution	No. of Institutions: Total No.	No. of Institutions: No. per 10 lakh of population	No. of Inhabitants served by one Institution
1.	Pre-Primary/Pre-Basic School	328	834.03	1,199
2.	Primary/Junior Basic School	482	1,225.49	816
3.	Middle/Senior Basic School	122	310.27	3,223
4.	High/Post-Basic School	54	137.34	7,281
5.	Higher Secondary Old Pattern School	—	—	—
6.	Higher Secondary (10+2) Institution	13	33.06	30,246
7.	Intermediate/Junior College	—	—	—
8.	Board of Intermediate/Secondary Education	—	—	—
9.	Teacher Training College	—	—	—
10.	Teacher Training School	1	2.54	3,93,200
11.	Polytechnic Institute	—	—	—
12.	Technical Industrial Arts/Crafts School	1	2.54	3,93,200
13.	Arts/Science/Commerce College	1	2.54	3,93,200
14.	Engineering & Technical College	—	—	—
15.	Medical College	—	—	—
16.	Universities	—	—	—

Sl. No.	Category of Enrolment	No. of Students enrolled: Total No.	No. of Students enrolled: No. per 10,000 of Population	No. of Inhabitants per student enrolled
1.	Pre-Primary/Pre-Basic Stage	8,973	227.27	44
2.	Primary Stage (Class I-V)	65,623	1,666.67	6
3.	Middle/Senior Basic Stage (VI-VIII)	16,110	416.67	24
4.	High/Post-Basic Stage (IX-X)	4,247	108.70	92.5
5.	Higher Secondary Old Pattern	—	—	—
6.	Higher Secondary (10+2)	1,187	30.21	331
7.	Pre-University	—	—	—
8.	Pre-Degree/Pre-University	—	—	—
9.	Intermediate/Junior College	—	—	—
10.	B.A./B.A. (Hons.)	273	6.94	1,440
11.	B.Sc./B.Sc. (Hons.)	98	2.49	4,012
12.	B.Com./B.Com. (Hons.)	77	1.96	5,106
13.	M.A.	—	—	—
14.	M.Sc.	—	—	—
15.	M.Com.	—	—	—
16	Ph.D.	—	—	—
17.	B.Ed./B.T.	—	—	—
18.	B.E./B.Sc.(Engg.)/B.Architect	—	—	—
19.	M.B.B.S.	—	—	—

TABLE 5.19: **Tamilnadu Population: 5,34,12,400**

Sl. No.	*Type of Institution*	*No. of Institutions*		*No. of Inhabitants served by one Institution*
		Total No.	*No. per 10 lakh of population*	
1.	Pre-Primary/Pre-Basic School	26	0.49	20,54,323
2.	Primary/Junior Basic School	29,268	547.95	1,825
3.	Middle/Senior Basic School	5,665	106.07	9,428
4.	High/Post-Basic School	2,688	50.32	19,871
5.	Higher Secondary Old Pattern School	—	—	—
6.	Higher Secondary (10+2) Institution	1,678	31.42	31,831
7.	Intermediate/Junior College	—		
8.	Board of Intermediate/Secondary Education	5	0.09	1,06,82,480
9.	Teacher Training College	22	0.41	24,27,836
10.	Teacher Training School	79	1.48	6,76,106
11.	Polytechnic Institute	135	2.53	3,95,647
12.	Technical Industrial Arts/Crafts School	110	2.06	4,85,567
13.	Arts/Science/Commerce College	198	3.71	2,69,760
14.	Engineering & Technical College	38	0.71	14,05,589
15.	Medical College	9	0.17	59,34,711
16.	Universities	12	0.22	44,51,033

Sl. No.	*Category of Enrolment*	*No. of Students enrolled*		*No. of Inhabitants per student enrolled*
		Total No.	*No. per 10,000 of Population*	
1.	Pre-Primary/Pre-Basic Stage	4,648	0.87	11,491.48
2.	Primary Stage (Class I-V)	73,28,105	1,373.60	7.28
3.	Middle/Senior Basic Stage (VI-VIII)	26,16,015	490	20.4
4.	High/Post-Basic Stage (IX-X)	9,70,216	181.65	55.05
5.	Higher Secondary Old Pattern	—	—	—
6.	Higher Secondary (10+2)	3,61,662	67.75	147.68
7.	Pre-University	—	—	—
8.	Pre-Degree/Pre-University	—	—	—
9.	Intermediate/Junior College	—	—	—
10.	B.A./B.A. (Hons.)	60,938	11.40	876.50
11.	B.Sc./B.Sc. (Hons.)	82,938	15.52	644
12.	B.Com./B.Com. (Hons.)	33,894	6.34	1,575.8
13.	M.A.	8,167	1.53	6,540
14.	M.Sc.	8,172	1.53	6,536
15.	M.Com.	2,736	0.51	19,522
16.	Ph.D.	1,954	0.36	27,334.90
17.	B.Ed./B.T.	2,888	0.54	18,494.5
18.	B.E./B.Sc.(Engg.)/B.Architect	19,769	3.7	2,701.2
19.	M.B.B.S.	6,889	1.29	7,753.20

TABLE 5.20: **Tripura: Population: 23,80,300**

Sl. No.	*Type of Institution*	*No. of Institutions*		*No. of Inhabitants served by one Institution*
		Total No.	*No. per 10 lakh of population*	
1.	Pre-Primary/Pre-Basic School	—	—	—
2.	Primary/Junior Basic School	1,956	821.69	1,217
3.	Middle/Senior Basic School	328	137.80	7,257
4.	High/Post-Basic School	173	72.68	13,759
5.	Higher Secondary Old Pattern School	—	—	—
6.	Higher Secondary (10+2) Institution	92	38.65	25,873
7.	Intermediate/Junior College	—	—	—
8.	Board of Intermediate/Secondary Education	1	0.42	23,80,300
9.	Teacher Training College	—	—	—
10.	Teacher Training School	—	—	—
11.	Polytechnic Institute	1	0.42	23,80,300
12.	Technical Industrial Arts/Crafts School	3	1.26	7,93,433
13.	Arts/Science/Commerce College	9	3.78	2,64,478
14.	Engineering & Technical College	1	0.42	23,80,300
15.	Medical College	—	—	
16.	Universities	1	0.42	23,80,300

Sl. No.	*Category of Enrolment*	*No. of Students enrolled*		*No. of Inhabitants per student enrolled*
		Total No.	*No. per 10,000 of Population*	
1.	Pre-Primary/Pre-Basic Stage	95,726	400.00	25
2.	Primary Stage (Class I-V)	3,08,260	1,250.00	8
3.	Middle/Senior Basic Stage (VI-VIII)	81,684	343.60	29.1
4.	High/Post-Basic Stage (IX-X)	32,888	138.89	72
5.	Higher Secondary Old Pattern	—	—	—
6.	Higher Secondary (10+2)	14,973	62.89	159
7.	Pre-University	—	—	—
8.	Pre-Degree/Pre-University	—	—	—
9.	Intermediate/Junior College	—	—	—
10.	B.A./B.A. (Hons.)	4,920	20.66	484
11.	B.Sc./B.Sc. (Hons.)	1,302	5.47	1,828
12.	B.Com./B.Com. (Hons.)	1,653	6.94	1,440
13.	M.A.	72	0.30	33,060
14.	M.Sc.	45	0.19	52,896
15.	M.Com.	—	—	—
16.	Ph.D.	—	—	—
17.	B.Ed./B.T.	132	0.55	18,033
18.	B.E./B.Sc.(Engg.)/B.Architect	416	1.75	5,722
19.	M.B.B.S.	—	—	

TABLE 5.21: **Uttar Pradesh: Population: 12,54,80,100**

Sl. No.	*Type of Institution*	*No. of Institutions*		*No. of Inhabitants served by one Institution*
		Total No.	*No. per 10 lakh of population*	
1.	Pre-Primary/Pre-Basic School	27	0:22	46,47,411
2.	Primary/Junior Basic School	74,273	592.07	1,689
3.	Middle/Senior Basic School	16,504	131.53	7,603
4.	High/Post-Basic School	2,361	18.82	53,147
5.	Higher Secondary Old Pattern School	—	—	—
6.	Higher Secondary (10+2) Institution	—	—	—
7.	Intermediate/Junior College	3,330	26.54	37,682
8.	Board of Intermediate/Secondary Education	1	0.01	12,54,80,100
9.	Teacher Training College	13	0.10	96,52,315
10.	Teacher Training School	121	0.96	10,37,026
11.	Polytechnic Institute	48	0.38	26,14,169
12.	Technical Industrial Arts/Crafts School	78	0.62	16,08,719
13.	Arts/Science/Commerce College	404	3.22	3,10,594
14.	Engineering & Technical College	3	0.02	4,18,26,700
15.	Medical College	8	0.06	1,56,85,013
16.	Universities	24	0.19	52,28,338

Sl. No.	*Category of Enrolment*	*No. of Students enrolled*		*No. of Inhabitants per student enrolled*
		Total No.	*No. per 10,000 of Population*	
1.	Pre-Primary/Pre-Basic Stage	33,297	2.65	3,769
2.	Primary Stage (Class I-V)	1,23,32,663	983.00	10.17
3.	Middle/Senior Basic Stage (VI-VIII)	39,51,904	312.50	32
4.	High/Post-Basic Stage (IX-X)	18,69,905	149.25	67
5.	Higher Secondary Old Pattern	—	—	—
6.	Higher Secondary (10+2)	—	—	—
7.	Pre-University	3,674	0.29	34,154
8.	Pre-Degree/Pre-University	—	—	—
9.	Intermediate/Junior College	6,77,699	54.05	185
10.	B.A./B.A.(Hons.)	2,31,144	18.4	542.2
11.	B.Sc./B.Sc.(Hons.)	61,932	4.94	2,026
12.	B.Com./B.Com. (Hons.)	36,658	2.92	3,423
13.	M.A.	61,438	4.90	2,041
14.	M.Sc.	13,833	1.10	9,071
15.	M.Com.	8,366	0.70	14,998.80
16.	Ph.D.	7,743	0.62	16,206
17.	B.Ed./B.T.	16,060	1.28	7,813
18.	B.E./B.Sc.(Engg.)/B.Architect	14,037	1.12	8,939
19.	M.B.B.S.	6,807	0.54	18,434

TABLE 5.22: **West Bengal: Population: 6,13,77,000**

Sl. No.	Type of Institution	No. of Institutions		No. of Inhabitants served by one Institution
		Total No.	No. per 10 lakh of population	
1.	Pre-Primary/Pre-Basic School	192	3.13	3,19,672
2.	Primary/Junior Basic School	50811	827.81	1,208
3.	Middle/Senior Basic School	3933	64.08	15,606
4.	High/Post-Basic School	5614	91.47	10,933
5.	Higher Secondary Old Pattern School	—	—	—
6.	Higher Secondary (10+2) Institution	1,140	18.57	53,839
7.	Intermediate/Junior College	268	4.37	2,29,019
8.	Board of Intermediate/Secondary Education	2	0.03	3,06,88,500
9.	Teacher Training College	43	0.70	14,27,372
10.	Teacher Training School	57	0.93	1076,789
11.	Polytechnic Institute	—	—	—
12.	Technical Industrial Arts/Crafts School	149	2.43	4,11,926
13.	Arts/Science/Commerce College	302	4.92	2,03,235
14.	Engineering & Technical College	9	0.15	68;19,667
15.	Medical College	10	0.16	61,37,700
16.	Universities	11	0.18	55,79,727

Sl. No.	Category of Enrolment	No. of Students enrolled		No. of Inhabitants per student enrolled
		Total No.	No. per 10,000 of Population	
1.	Pre-Primary/Pre-Basic Stage	33,793	5.51	1,816
2.	Primary Stage (Class I-V)	82,05,355	1428.57	7
3.	Middle/Senior Basic Stage (VI-VIII)	26,40,063	434.78	23
4.	High/Post-Basic Stage (IX-X)	10,56,656	172.41	58
5.	Higher Secondary Old Pattern	—	—	—
6.	Higher Secondary (10+2)	3,79,816	61.73	162
7.	Pre-University	—	—	—
8.	Pre-Degree/Pre-University	—	—	—
9.	Intermediate/Junior College	1,52,722	24.88	402
10.	B.A./B.A.(Hons.)	1,40,422	22.88	437
11.	B.Sc./B.Sc.(Hons.)	68,419	11.15	897
12.	B.Com./B.Com. (Hons.)	71,301	11.61	861
13.	M.A.	12,343	2.01	4,973
14.	M.Sc.	4,315	0.70	14,224
15.	M.Com.	2,564	0.42	23,938
16.	Ph.D.	1,302	0.21	47,141
17.	B.Ed./B.T.	9,524	1.55	6,444
18.	B.E./B.Sc.(Engg.)/B.Architect	7,650	1.25	8,023
19.	M.B.B.S.	3,476	0.57	17,657

6

UNION TERRITORY EDUCATION PROFILE

TABLE 6.1: **Andaman and Nicobar Islands: Population: 2,48,900**

Sl. No.	*Type of Institution*	*No. of Institutions*		*No. of Inhabitants served by one Institution*
		Total No.	*No. per 10 lakh of population*	
1.	Pre-Primary/Pre-Basic School	18	72.32	13,828
2.	Primary/Junior Basic School	184	739.10	1,353
3.	Middle/Senior Basic School	40	160.69	6,223
4.	High/Post-Basic School	23	92.40	10,822
5.	Higher Secondary Old Pattern School	—	—	—
6.	Higher Secondary (10+2) Institution	27	108.47	9,219
7.	Intermediate/Junior College	—	—	—
8.	Board of Intermediate/Secondary Education	—	—	—
9.	Teacher Training College	1	4.02	2,48,900
10.	Teacher Training School	1	4.02	2,48,000
11.	Polytechnic Institute	1	4.02	2,48,000
12.	Technical Industrial Arts/Crafts School	—	—	—
13.	Arts/Science/Commerce College	1	4.02	2,48,900
14.	Engineering & Technical College	—	—	—
15.	Medical College	—	—	—
16.	Universities	—	—	—

Sl. No.	*Category of Enrolment*	*No. of Students enrolled*		*No. of Inhabitants per student enrolled*
		Total No.	*No. per 10,000 of Population*	
1.	Pre-Primary/Pre-Basic Stage	2,388	96.15	104
2.	Primary Stage (Class I-V)	35,110	1,428.57	7
3.	Middle/Senior Basic Stage (VI-VIII)	15,696	625.00	16
4.	High/Post-Basic Stage (IX-X)	6,836	274.78	36.4
5.	Higher Secondary Old Pattern	—	—	—
6.	Higher Secondary (10+2)	3,213	129.87	77
7.	Pre-University	—	—	—
8.	Pre-Degree/Pre-University	—	—	—
9.	Intermediate/Junior College	—	—	—
10.	B.A./B.A. (Hons.)	317	32.79	305
11.	B.Sc./B.Sc. (Hons.)	119	4.78	2,092
12.	B.Com./B.Com. (Hons.)	43	1.73	5,788
13.	M.A.	74	2.97	3,364
14.	M.Sc.	—	—	—
15.	M.Com.	—	—	—
16.	Ph.D.	—	—	—
17.	B.Ed./B.T.	50	2.01	4,978
18.	B.E./B.Sc.(Engg.)/B.Architect	—	—	—
19.	M.B.B.S.	—	—	—

TABLE 6.2: **Arunachal Pradesh: Population: 7,46,600**

Sl. No.	Type of Institution	No. of Institutions		No. of Inhabitants served by one Institution
		Total No.	No. per 10 lakh of population	
1.	Pre-Primary/Pre-Basic School	249	333.56	2,998
2.	Primary/Junior Basic School	1,039	1,390.82	719
3.	Middle/Senior Basic School	186	249.13	4,014
4.	High/Post-Basic School	49	65.63	15,237
5.	Higher Secondary Old Pattern School	—	—	—
6.	Higher Secondary (10+2) Institution	32	42.86	23,331
7.	Intermediate/Junior College	—	—	—
8.	Board of Intermediate/Secondary Education	—	—	—
9.	Teacher Training College	—	—	—
10.	Teacher Training School	—	—	—
11.	Polytechnic Institute	—	—	—
12.	Technical Industrial Arts/Crafts School	3	4.02	2,48,867
13.	Arts/Science/Commerce College	3	4.02	2,48,867
14.	Engineering & Technical College	—	—	—
15.	Medical College	—	—	—
16.	Universities	1	1.34	7,46,600

Sl. No.	Category of Enrolment	No. of Students enrolled		No. of Inhabitants per student enrolled
		Total No.	No. per 10,000 of Population	
1.	Pre-Primary/Pre-Basic Stage	9,034	120.48	83
2.	Primary Stage (Class I-V)	91,482	1,225.49	8.16
3.	Middle/Senior Basic Stage (VI-VIII)	2,13,339	2,865.3	3.49
4.	High/Post-Basic Stage (IX-X)	7,214	97.09	103
5.	Higher Secondary Old Pattern	—	—	—
6.	Higher Secondary (10+2)	2,507	33.56	298
7.	Pre-University	—	—	—
8.	Pre-Degree/Pre-University	—	—	—
9.	Intermediate/Junior College	—	—	—
10.	B.A./B.A.(Hons.)	911	12.20	820
11.	B.Sc./B.Sc.(Hons.)	91	1.22	8,204
12.	B.Com./B.Com. (Hons.)	36	0.48	20,739
13.	M.A.	42	0.56	17,776
14.	M.Sc.	—	—	—
15.	M.Com.	—	—	—
16.	Ph.D.	—	—	—
17.	B.Ed./B.T.	—	—	—
18.	B.E./B.Sc.(Engg.)/B.Architect	—	—	—
19.	M.B.B.S.	—	—	—

TABLE 6.3: **Chandigarh: Population: 6,18,200**

Sl. No.	Type of Institution	No. of Institutions: Total No.	No. of Institutions: No. per 10 lakh of population	No. of Inhabitants served by one Institution
1.	Pre-Primary/Pre-Basic School	33	53.38	18,733
2.	Primary/Junior Basic School	34	55.00	18,182
3.	Middle/Senior Basic School	28	45.29	22,079
4.	High/Post-Basic School	38	61.47	16,268
5.	Higher Secondary Old Pattern School	6	9.71	1,03,033
6.	Higher Secondary (10+2) Institution	—	—	—
7.	Intermediate/Junior College	—	—	—
8.	Board of Intermediate/Secondary Education	—	—	—
9.	Teacher Training College	—		—
10.	Teacher Training School	—	—	—
11.	Polytechnic Institute	2	3.24	3,09,100
12.	Technical Industrial Arts/Crafts School	2	3.24	3,09,100
13.	Arts/Science/Commerce College	12	19.41	51,517
14.	Engineering & Technical College	2	3.24	3,09,100
15.	Medical College	—	—	—
16.	Universities	1	1.62	6,18,200

Sl. No.	Category of Enrolment	No. of Students enrolled: Total No.	No. of Students enrolled: No. per 10,000 of Population	No. of Inhabitants per student enrolled
1.	Pre-Primary/Pre-Basic Stage	5,591	90.09	111
2.	Primary Stage (Class I-V)	30,353	486.38	20.36
3.	Middle/Senior Basic Stage (VI-VIII)	15,640	250.00	40
4.	High/Post-Basic Stage (IX-X)	6,467	104.17	96
5.	Higher Secondary Old Pattern	700	11.33	883
6.	Higher Secondary (10+2)	—	—	—
7.	Pre-University	21,803	357.14	28
8.	Pre-Degree/Pre-University	—	—	—
9.	Intermediate/Junior College	—	—	—
10.	B.A./B.A. (Hons.)	32,852	526.32	19
11.	B.Sc./B.Sc. (Hons.)	3,777	60.98	164
12.	B.Com./B.Com. (Hons.)	3,845	62.11	161
13.	M.A.	434	7.02	1,424
14.	M.Sc.	21,292	37.04	270
15.	M.Com.	172	2.78	3,594
16.	Ph.D.	—	—	—
17.	B.Ed./B.T.	2,568	41.49	241
18.	B.E./B.Sc.(Engg.)/B.Architect	2,222	35.97	278
19.	M.B.B.S.	527	8.53	1,173

TABLE 6.4: **Daman & Nagar Haveli: Population: 1,20,800**

Sl. No.	Type of Institution	No. of Institutions: Total No.	No. of Institutions: No. per 10 lakh of population	No. of Inhabitants served by one Institution
1.	Pre-Primary/Pre-Basic School	—	—	—
2.	Primary/Junior Basic School	124	1,026.69	974
3.	Middle/Senior Basic School	36	297.97	3,356
4.	High/Post-Basic School	4	33.11	30,200
5.	Higher Secondary Old Pattern School	—	—	—
6.	Higher Secondary (10+2) Institution	3	24.83	40,267
7.	Intermediate/Junior College	—	—	—
8.	Board of Intermediate/Secondary Education	—	—	—
9.	Teacher Training College	—	—	—
10.	Teacher Training School	—	—	—
11.	Polytechnic Institute	—	—	—
12.	Technical Industrial Arts/Crafts School	—	—	—
13.	Arts/Science/Commerce College	—	—	—
14.	Engineering & Technical College	—	—	—
15.	Medical College	—	—	—
16.	Universities	—	—	—

Sl. No.	Category of Enrolment	No. of Students enrolled: Total No.	No. of Students enrolled: No. per 10,000 of Population	No. of Inhabitants per student enrolled
1.	Pre-Primary/Pre-Basic Stage	—	—	—
2.	Primary Stage (Class I-V)	14,475	1,199.04	8.34
3.	Middle/Senior Basic Stage (VI-VIII)	3,753	312.50	32
4.	High/Post-Basic Stage (IX-X)	1,552	128.21	78
5.	Higher Secondary Old Pattern	—	—	—
6.	Higher Secondary (10+2)	182	15.06	664
7.	Pre-University	—	—	—
8.	Pre-Degree/Pre-University	—	—	—
9.	Intermediate/Junior College	—	—	—
10.	B.A./B.A.(Hons.)	—	—	—
11.	B.Sc./B.Sc.(Hons.)	—	—	—
12.	B.Com./B.Com. (Hons.)	—	—	—
13.	M.A.	—	—	—
14.	M.Sc.	—	—	—
15.	M.Com.	—	—	—
16.	Ph.D.	—	—	—
17.	B.Ed./B.T.	—	—	—
18.	B.E./B.Sc.(Engg.)/B.Architect	—	—	—
19.	M.B.B.S.	—	—	—

TABLE 6.5: **Delhi: Population: 79,09,500**

Sl. No.	*Type of Institution*	*No. of Institutions*		*No. of Inhabitants served by one Institution*
		Total No.	*No. per 10 lakh of population*	
1.	Pre-Primary/Pre-Basic School	51	6.45	1,55,088
2.	Primary/Junior Basic School	1,832	231.64	4,317
3.	Middle/Senior Basic School	360	45.51	21,971
4.	High/Post-Basic School	258	32.62	30,657
5.	Higher Secondary Old Pattern School	—	—	—
6.	Higher Secondary (10+2) Institution	663	83.82	11,930
7.	Intermediate/Junior College	—	—	—
8.	Board of Intermediate/Secondary Education	1	0.13	79,09,500
9.	Teacher Training College	—	—	—
10.	Teacher Training School	5	0.63	15,81,900
11.	Polytechnic Institute	5	0.63	15,81,900
12.	Technical Industrial Arts/Crafts School	15	1.90	5,27,300
13.	Arts/Science/Commerce College	52	6.57	1,52,106
14.	Engineering & Technical College	2	0.25	39,54,750
15.	Medical College	4	0.51	19,77,375
16.	Universities	7	0.89	11,29,929

Sl. No.	*Category of Enrolment*	*No. of Students enrolled*		*No. of Inhabitants per student enrolled*
		Total No.	*No. per 10,000 of Population*	
1.	Pre-Primary/Pre-Basic Stage	55,540	70.42	142
2.	Primary Stage (Class I-V)	8,33,034	1,053.74	9.49
3.	Middle/Senior Basic Stage (VI-VIII)	4,41,599	555.56	18
4.	High/Post-Basic Stage (IX-X)	2,11,253	270.27	37
5.	Higher Secondary Old Pattern	—	—	—
6.	Higher Secondary (10+2)	1,20,530	151.52	66
7.	Pre-University	—	—	—
8.	Pre-Degree/Pre-University	—	—	—
9.	Intermediate/Junior College	—	—	—
10.	B.A./B.A. (Hons.)	56,070	70.92	141
11.	B.Sc./B.Sc. (Hons.)	13,600	17.18	582
12.	B.Com./B.Com. (Hons.)	29,775	37.59	266
13.	M.A.	5,540	7.00	1,428
14.	M.Sc.	1,550	1.96	5,103
15.	M.Com.	1,259	1.59	6,282
16.	Ph.D.	5,303	6.70	1,492
17.	B.Ed./B.T.	728	0.92	10,865
18.	B.E./B.Sc.(Engg.)/B.Architect	3,926	4.96	2,015
19.	M.B.B.S.	4,085	5.17	1,936

TABLE 6.6: **Goa Daman & Diu: Population: 12,53,800**

Sl. No.	*Type of Institution*	*No. of Institutions*		*No. of Inhabitants served by one Institution*
		Total No.	*No. per 10 lakh of population*	
1.	Pre-Primary/Pre-Basic School	495	394.79	2,533
2.	Primary/Junior Basic School	1,014	809.06	1,236
3.	Middle/Senior Basic School	139	110.86	9,020
4.	High/Post-Basic School	313	249.63	4,006
5.	Higher Secondary Old Pattern School	—	—	—
6.	Higher Secondary (10+2) Institution	25	19.94	50,152
7.	Intermediate/Junior College	—	—	—
8.	Board of Intermediate/Secondary Education	1	0.80	12,53,800
9.	Teacher Training College	1	0.80	12,53,800
10.	Teacher Training School	5	3.99	2,50,760
11.	Polytechnic Institute	3	2.39	4,17,933
12.	Technical Industrial Arts/Crafts School	18	14.36	69,656
13.	Arts/Science/Commerce College	11	8.77	1,13,982
14.	Engineering & Technical College	2	1.60	6,26,900
15.	Medical College	1	0.80	12,53,800
16.	Universities	1	0.80	12,53,800

Sl. No.	*Category of Enrolment*	*No. of Students enrolled*		*No. of Inhabitants per student enrolled*
		Total No.	*No. per 10,000 of Population*	
1.	Pre-Primary/Pre-Basic Stage	—	—	—
2.	Primary Stage (Class I-V)	1,63,862	1,307.18	7.65
3.	Middle/Senior Basic Stage (VI-VIII)	83,146	663.57	15.07
4.	High/Post-Basic Stage (IX-X)	35,155	277.78	36
5.	Higher Secondary Old Pattern	—	—	—
6.	Higher Secondary.(10+2)	13,184	105.26	95
7.	Pre-University	—	—	—
8.	Pre-Degree/Pre-University	—	—	—
9.	Intermediate/Junior College	—	—	—
10.	B.A./B.A.(Hons.)	1,890	15.08	663
11.	B.Sc./B.Sc.(Hons.)	1,459	11.64	859
12.	B.Com./B.Com. (Hons.)	3,792	30.21	331
13.	M.A.	166	1.32	7,553
14.	M.Sc.	127	1.01	9,872
15.	M.Com.	126	1.00	9,951
16.	Ph.D.	57	0.45	21,996
17.	B.Ed./B.T.	103	0.82	12,173
18.	B.E./B.Sc.(Engg.)/B.Architect	517	4.12	2,425
19.	M.B.B.S	395	3.15	3,174

TABLE 6.7: **Lakshdweep: Population: 44,000**

Sl. No.	Type of Institution	No. of Institutions		No. of Inhabitants served by one Institution
		Total No.	No. per 10 lakh of population	
1.	Pre-Primary/Pre-Basic School	20	454.55	2,200
2.	Primary/Junior Basic School	19	431.78	2,316
3.	Middle/Senior Basic School	4	90.91	11,000
4.	High/Post-Basic School	9	204.54	4,889
5.	Higher Secondary Old Pattern School	—	—	—
6.	Higher Secondary (10+2) Institution	—	—	—
7.	Intermediate/Junior College	2	45.45	22,000
8.	Board of Intermediate/Secondary Education	—	—	—
9.	Teacher Training College	—	—	—
10.	Teacher Training School	—	—	—
11.	Polytechnic Institute	—	—	—
12.	Technical Industrial Arts/Crafts School	—	—	—
13.	Arts/Science/Commerce College	—	—	—
14.	Engineering & Technical College	—	—	—
15.	Medical College	—	—	—
16.	Universities	—	—	—

Sl. No.	Category of Enrolment	No. of Students enrolled		No. of Inhabitants per student enrolled
		Total No.	No. per 10,000 of Population	
1.	Pre-Primary/Pre-Basic Stage	1,304	294.12	34
2.	Primary Stage (Class I-V)	8,139	1,851.85	5.4
3.	Middle/Senior Basic Stage (VI-VIII)	3,009	684.93	14.6
4.	High/Post-Basic Stage (IX-X)	1,203	270.27	37
5.	Higher Secondary Old Pattern	—	—	—
6.	Higher Secondary (10+2)	—	—	—
7.	Pre-University	—	—	—
8.	Pre-Degree/Pre-University	422	96.15	104
9.	Intermediate/Junior College	—	—	—
10.	B.A./B.A.(Hons.)	—	—	—
11.	B.Sc./B.Sc.(Hons.)	—	—	—
12.	B.Com./B.Com. (Hons.)	—	—	—
13.	M.A.	—	—	—
14.	M.Sc.	—	—	—
15.	M.Com.	—	—	—
16.	Ph.D.	—	—	—
17.	B.Ed./B.T.	—	—	—
18.	B.E./B.Sc.(Engg.)/B.Architect	—	—	—
19.	M.B.B.S.	—	—	—

TABLE 5.8: **Mizoram: Population: 6,22,100**

Sl. No.	*Type of Institution*	*No. of Institutions*		*No. of Inhabitants served by one Institution*
		Total No	*No. per 10 lakh of population*	
1.	Pre-Primary/Pre-Basic School	—	—	—
2.	Primary/Junior Basic School	1,000	1,607.72	622
3.	Middle/Senior Basic School	437	702.25	1,424
4.	High/Post-Basic School	149	239.52	4,175
5.	Higher Secondary Old Pattern School	—	—	—
6.	Higher Secondary (10+2) Institution	—	—	—
7.	Intermediate/Junior College	—	—	—
8.	Board of Intermediate/Secondary Education	—	—	—
9.	Teacher Training College	1	1.61	6,22,100
10.	Teacher Training School	2	3.21	3,11,050
11.	Polytechnic Institute	1	1.61	6,22,100
12.	Technical Industrial Arts/Crafts School	1	1.61	6,22,100
13.	Arts/Science/Commerce College	12	19.29	51,842
14.	Engineering & Technical College	1	1.61	6,22,100
15.	Medical College	—	—	—
16.	Universities	—	—	—

Sl. No.	*Category of Enrolment*	*No. of Students enrolled*		*No. of Inhabitants per student enrolled*
		Total No.	*No. per 10,000 of Population*	
1.	Pre-Primary/Pre-Basic Stage	3,803	60.98	164
2.	Primary Stage (Class I-V)	97,084	1,562.5	6.4
3.	Middle/Senior Basic Stage (VI-VIII)	27,721	454.5[illegible]	22
4.	High/Post-Basic Stage (IX-X)	9,530	153.85	65
5.	Higher Secondary Old Pattern	—	—	—
6.	Higher Secondary (10+2)	—	—	—
7.	Pre-University	—	—	—
8.	Pre-Degree/Pre-University	3,062	49.26	203
9.	Intermediate/Junior College	—	—	—
10.	B.A./B.A.(Hons.)	1,620	26.04	384
11.	B.Sc./B.Sc.(Hons.)	[illegible]27	2.04	4,898
12.	B.Com./B.Com. (Hons.)	112	1.80	5,554
13.	M.A.	23	0.37	27,048
14.	M.Sc.	—	—	—
15.	M.Com.	—	—	—
16.	Ph.D.	—	—	—
17.	B.Ed./B.T.	100	1.61	6,221
18.	B.E./B.Sc.(Engg.)/B.Architect	—	—	—
19.	M.B.B.S.	—	—	—

TABLE 6.9: **Pondicherry: Population: 6,92,300**

Sl. No.	Type of Institution	No. of Institutions		No. of Inhabitants served by one Institution
		Total No.	No. per 10 lakh of population	
1.	Pre-Primary/Pre-Basic School	110	158.89	6,293.6
2.	Primary/Junior Basic School	356	514.2	1,944.6
3.	Middle/Senior Basic School	102	147.3	6,787.2
4.	High/Post-Basic School	66	95.3	10,489.3
5.	Higher Secondary Old Pattern School	—	—	—
6.	Higher Secondary (10+2) Institution	21	30.3	32,966.6
7.	Intermediate/Junior College	1	1.4	6,92,300.0
8.	Board of Intermediate/Secondary Education	—	—	—
9.	Teacher Training College	1	1.4	6,92,300.0
10.	Teacher Training School	—	—	—
11.	Polytechnic Institute	3	4.3	2,30,766.6
12.	Technical Industrial Arts/Crafts School	—	—	—
13.	Arts/Science/Commerce College	6	8.6	1,15,383.3
14.	Engineering & Technical College	1	1.4	6,92,300.0
15.	Medical College	1	1.4	6,92,300.0
16.	Universities	1	1.4	6,92,300.0

Sl. No.	Category of Enrolment	No. of Students enrolled		No. of Inhabitants per student enrolled
		Total No.	No. per 10,000 of Population.	
1.	Pre-Primary/Pre-Basic Stage	6,087	87.72	114
2.	Primary Stage (Class I-V)	93,329	1,351.35	7.4
3.	Middle/Senior Basic Stage (VI-VIII)	45,574	658.3	15.19
4.	High/Post-Basic Stage (IX-X)	17,119	250.00	40
5.	Higher Secondary Old Pattern	—	—	—
6.	Higher Secondary (10+2)	5,636	81.30	123
7.	Pre-University	—	—	—
8.	Pre-Degree/Pre-University	580	8.38	1,194
9.	Intermediate/Junior College	320	4.62	2,163
10.	B.A./B.A.(Hons.)	411	5.94	1,684
11.	B.Sc./B.Sc.(Hons.)	461	6.66	1,502
12.	B.Com./B.Com. (Hons.)	163	2.35	4,247
13.	M.A.	64	0.92	10,817
14.	M.Sc.	48	0.69	14,423
15.	M.Com.	14	0.20	49,450
16.	Ph.D.			
17.	B.Ed./B.T.			
18.	B.E./B.Sc.(Engg.)/B.Architect	239	3.45	2,897
19.	M.B.B.S.	566	8.18	1,223

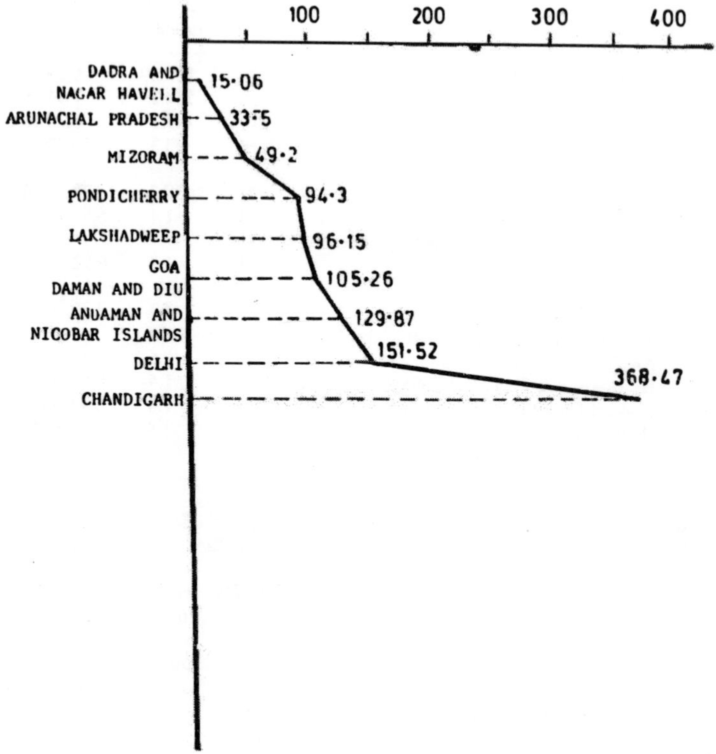

FIG. 6.1: Enrolment at Higher Secondary/Pre-University/Intermediate Level

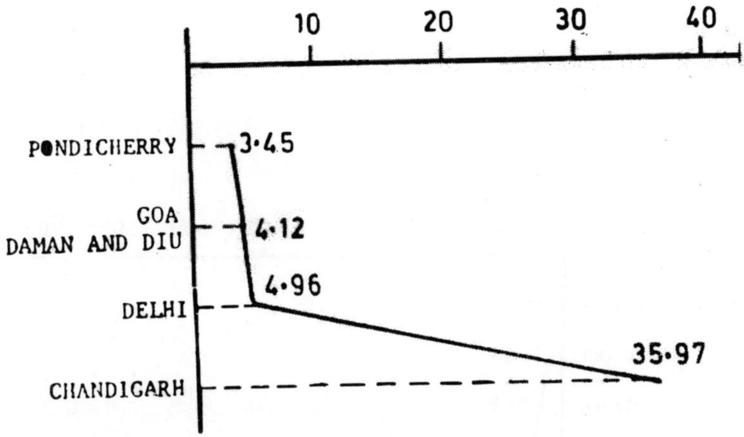

FIG. 6.2 : Enrolment in B.E./B.Sc. ENGG. Per 10,000 Population

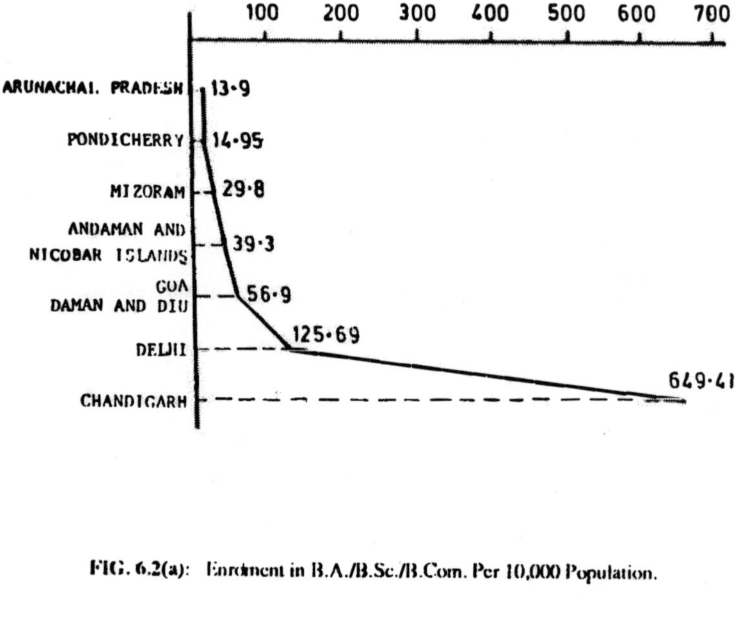

FIG. 6.2(a): Enrolment in B.A./B.Sc./B.Com. Per 10,000 Population.

7

ALL INDIA EDUCATION PROFILE

TABLE 7.1: **Enrolment (by Classes) in India**

Sl.No.	*Type/Class*	*Boys*	*Girls*	*Total*
1.	I-V	5,38,50,028	3,61,43,018	8,99,92,046
2.	VI-VIII	1,85,43,453	1,02,36,646	2,87,80,099
3.	High/Post-Basic IX, X	86,21,512	38,51,420	1,24,72,932
4.	Higher Secondary (Old Pattern)	1,28,174	32,708	1,60,882
5.	Higher Secondary (New Pattern 10+2)	19,26,850	9,40,500	28,67,385
6.	One Year Course (Pre-degree)	50,481	26,630	77,471
7.	Two Year Course (Pre-degree)	1,74,546	1,37,112	3,11,658
8.	Intermediate/Junior College	12,80,706	3,97,662	16,78,368
9.	Teacher Training School	46,984	45,901	92,885
10.	Polytechnic Institutions	1,64,454	34,088	1,98,542
11.	Technical Industrial/Art and Craft School	2,33,640	74,639	3,08,279
12.	B.Ed./B.T.	50,408	38,744	89,152
13.	M.B.B.S.	53,440	25,327	78,767
14.	B.E./B.Sc (Engg.)/B.Arch	1,59,629	22,792	1,82,421
15.	B.Com/B.Com (Hons.)	6,00,973	1,69,269	7,70,242
16.	B.Sc./B.Sc. (Hons.)	4,64,037	2,07,851	6,71,888
17.	B.A./B.A. (Hons.)	8,57,399	5,47,997	14,05,396
18.	M.Com.	52,882	9,100	61,982
19.	M.Sc.	52,816	26,315	79,131
20.	M.A.	1,19,309	71,777	1,91,086
21.	Ph.D./D.Sc./D.Ph.	21,068	10,465	31,533

TABLE 7.2. **Category and Number of Institutions in India**

Sl. No.	*Type*	*Number*
1.	Primary/Junior Basic Schools	5,37,399
2.	Middle/Senior Basic Schools	1,37,196
3.	High/Post-Basic Schools	53,172
4.	Higher Secondary/Old Pattern	898
5.	Higher Secondary New Pattern (10+2)	10,170
6.	Intermediate/Junior Colleges	4,655
7.	Polytechnic Institutes	713
8.	Technical Industrial/Art and Craft Schools	3,386
9.	Teacher Training Schools	973
10.	Teacher Training Colleges	462
11.	Medical Colleges (MBBS) only	117
12.	Engineering and Technology Colleges	225
13.	Arts, Science and Commerce Colleges	4,151
14.	Research Institutions	50
15.	Boards of Intermediate/Secondary Education	34
16.	Institutions of National Importance	10
17	Institutions Deemed Universities	17
18.	Universities	130

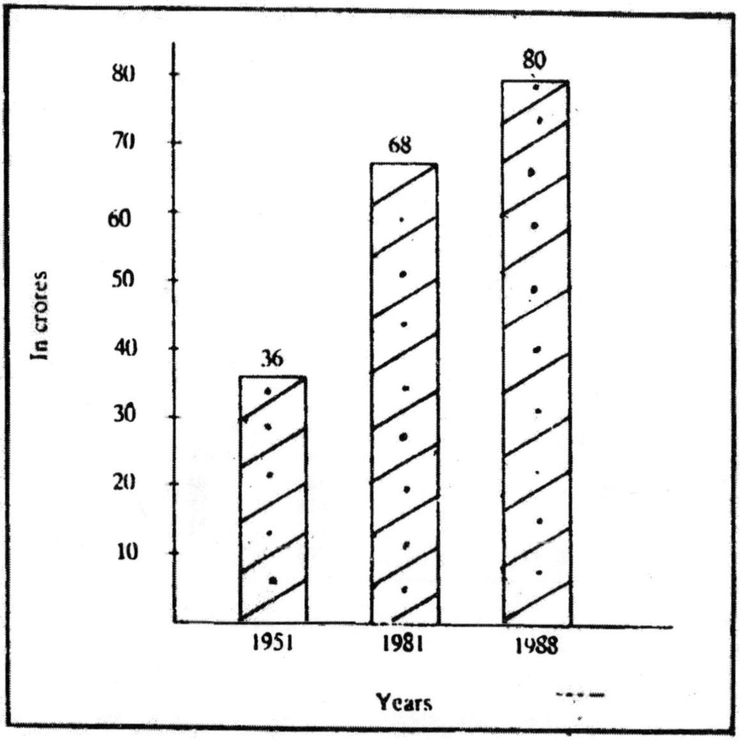

FIG. 7.1 : Population in India: 1951 to 1988.

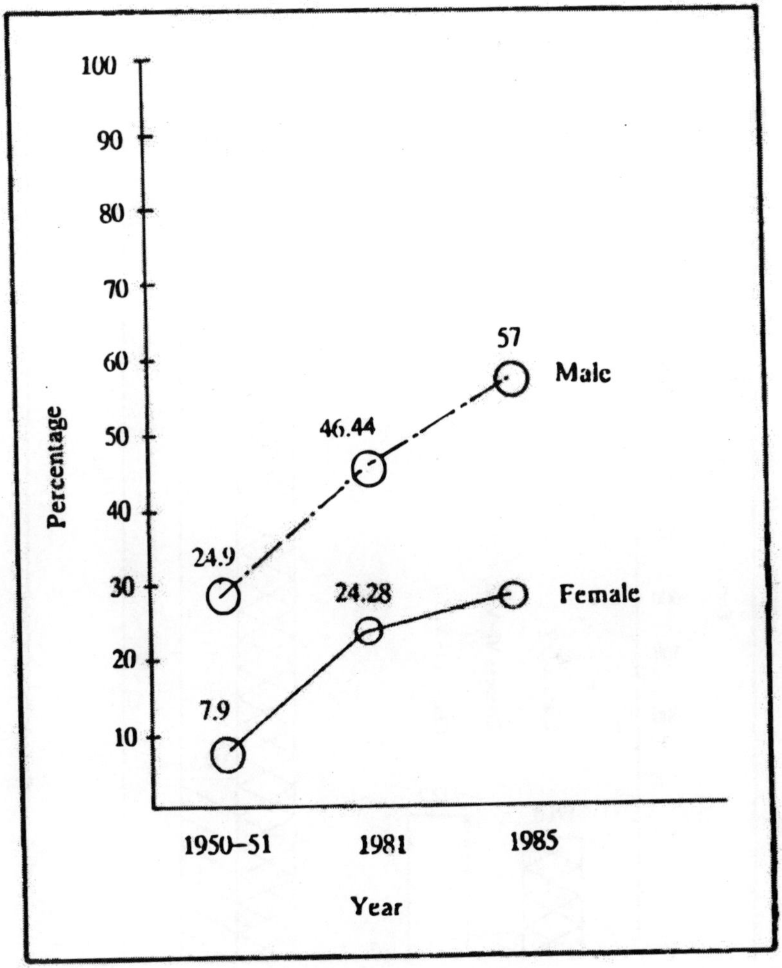

FIG. 7.2: Literacy Rate, 1950-51, 1981, 1985.

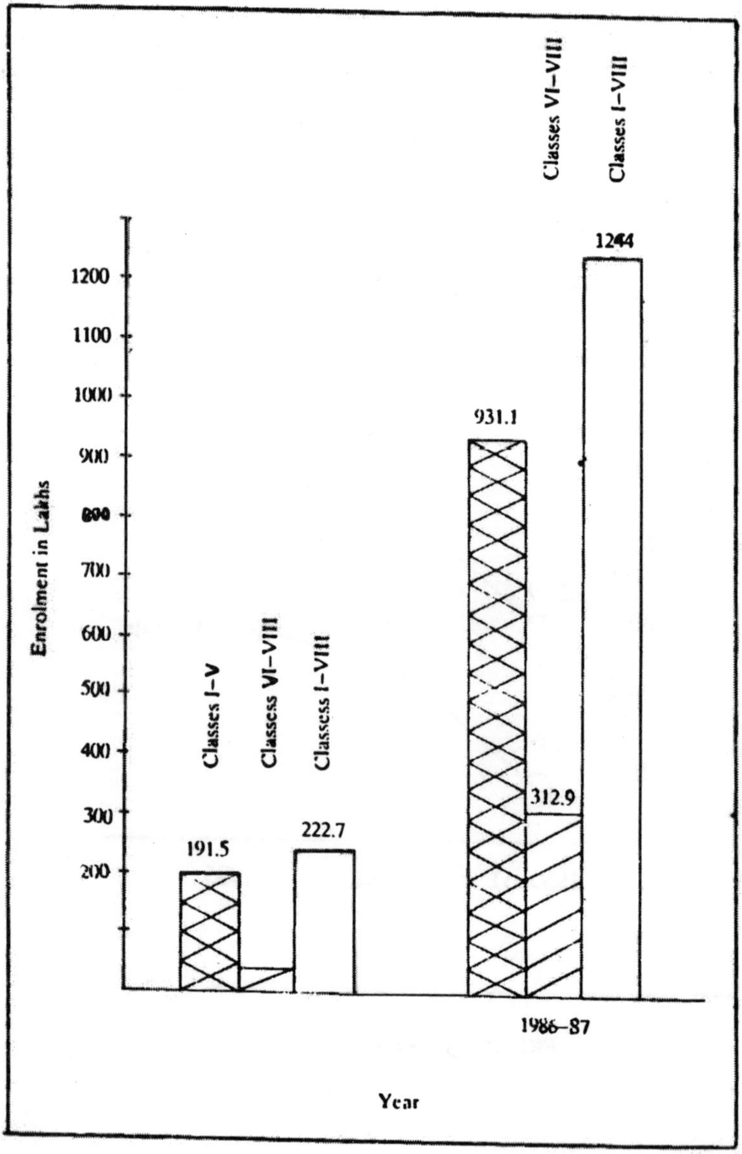

FIG. 7.3 : Elementary Education, 1950-51 and 1986-87.

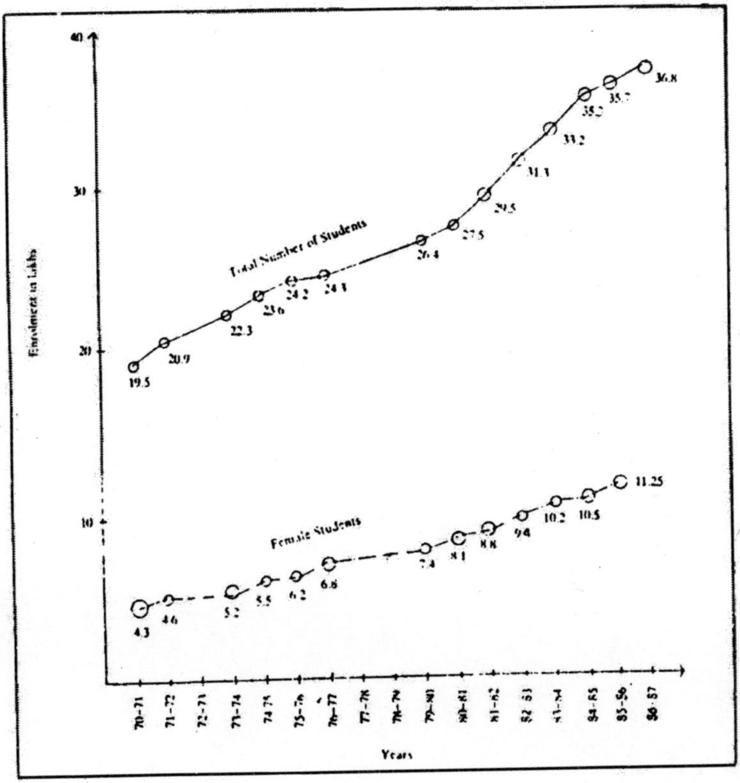

FIG. 7.4 : Women Higher Education

8

DEVELOPMENT OF EDUCATION IN INDIA PLAN PERIOD 1950-51 TO 1986-87

TABLE 8.1 **Sector-wise Plan/Non-Plan Revised Estimates for Education Departments of States/Union Territories and Centre (Revenue Account) for 1986-87**

(Rupees in Millions)

Sl. No.	*Sector*	*Total State/ Union Territories*	*Centre*	*Total*	*% of Plan Exp.*	*% of Non-Plan Exp.*	*% of Total Budget*
1.	Primary Education	34911.01	316.5	35227.6	35.3	44.5	43.3
2.	Secondary Education	24329.5	1347.5	25677.0	20.2	33.3	31.5
3.	Special Education	930.1	799.3	1729.4	10.7	0.8	2.1
4.	University and other Higher Education	9574.0	2129.5	11703.5	15.2	14.2	14.4
5.	Technical Education	2135.4	1579.2	3714.6	11.7	-3.5	4.6
6.	Sports and Youth Welfare	1048.7	16.6	1065.3	2.4	1.2	1.3
7.	Other Educational Programmes	1913.4	397.5	2310.9	4.5	2.5	2.8
	Total	74842.2	6586.1	81428.3	100.00	100.0	100.0

Source: Development of Education, 1986-88, National Report of India, National Institute of Educational Planning and Administration, Government of India, New Delhi.

TABLE 8.2: **Growth of Educational Institutions**

	1950-51	*1960-61*	*1970-71*	*1980-81*	*1986-87*
Number of Primary Schools (000's)	210	330	408	494	537
Number of Middle Schools (000's)	14	50	91	119	137
Number of Secondary/Higher Secondary Schools (000's)	7	17	37	51	69
Number of Colleges for General Education (Degree Standard & above)	542	1082	2285	3421	4151
Number of Colleges for Professional Education (Degree & above level)	182	810	992	1138	1280*

* Relates to 1982-83.

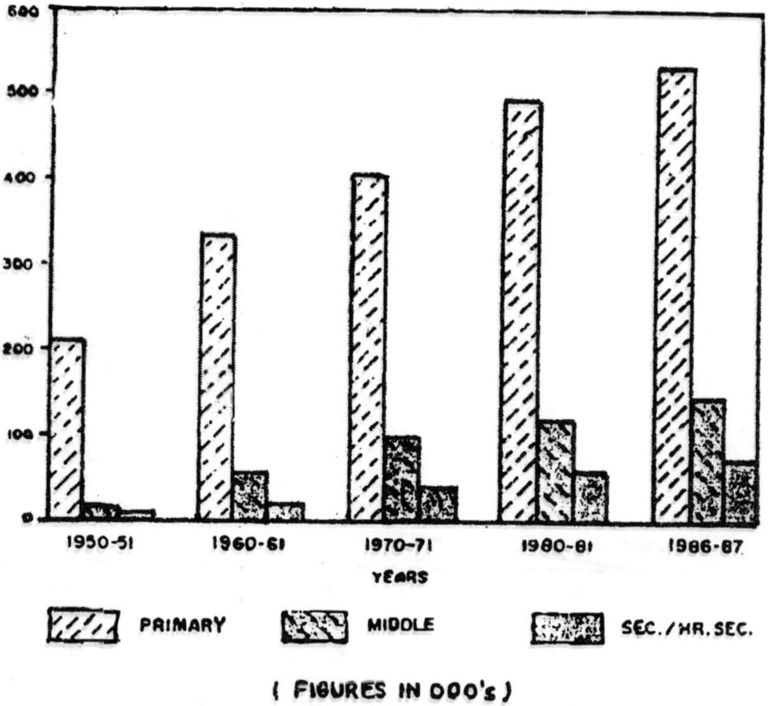

FIG. 8.1 : Growth of Educational Institutions (Schools)

TABLE 8.3: **Number of Students by Education Stage**

	1950-51	1960-61	1970-71	1980-81	1986-87
Num. of pupils in classes (Lakh)					
Primary I-V	192 (43.1)	350 (62.4)	570 (72.6)	738 (80.5)	900 (96.0)
Middle (VI-VIII)	31 (12.9)	67 (22.5)	133 (34.2)	207 (41.9)	288 (53.14)
Secondary (IX-XI/XII)	14	33	76	119	176
No. of pupils studying in degree level & above courses (Lakh)	2	6	25	30	34

Note: Figures in parentheses indicate percentage of enrolment to total population in the age group of 6-11 and 11-14 years.

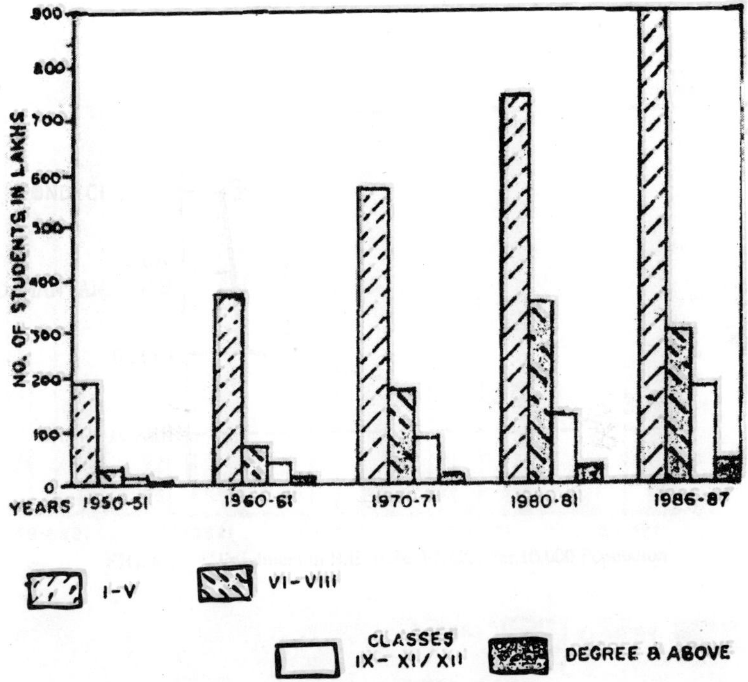

FIG. 8.2 : Growth of Enrolment

TABLE 8.4: **Girls' Enrolment by Stages**

(In Lakhs)

Stage	*1950-51*	*1960-61*	*1970-71*	*1980-81*	*1986-87*
Primary (I-V)	54	114	213	285	361
	(28.1)	(32.6)	(37.4)	(38.6)	(40.1)
Middle (VI-VIII)	5	16	39	88	102
	(16.1)	(23.9)	(29.3)	(32.9)	(35.4)
Secondary/Hr.Secondary/ 10+2/Intermediate	2	6	19	35	54
(IX & above)	(14.3)	(18.2)	(25.0)	(29.4)	(30.7)
Higher Education	.20	1	4	8	10*
(Degree & above level)	(10.0)	(16.7)	(20.0)	(26.7)	(29.4)

* Relates to 1982-83

Note : Figures in parentheses indicate percentage to total enrolment (Boys & Girls).

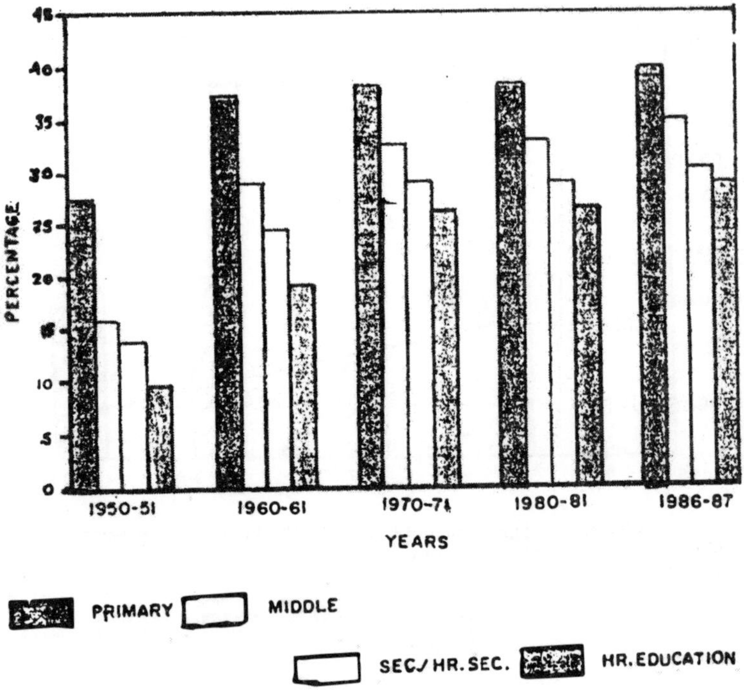

FIG. 8.3 : Percentage of Girls' Enrolment to Total Enrolment

TABLE 8.5: **Number of Teachers**

(In thousands)

	1950-51	*1960-61*	*1970-71*	*1980-81*	*1986-87*
Primary Schools	535	742	1060	1363	1522
Middle Schools	85	345	638	852	979
Secondary/Hr.Secondary Schools	127	296	629	912	1199

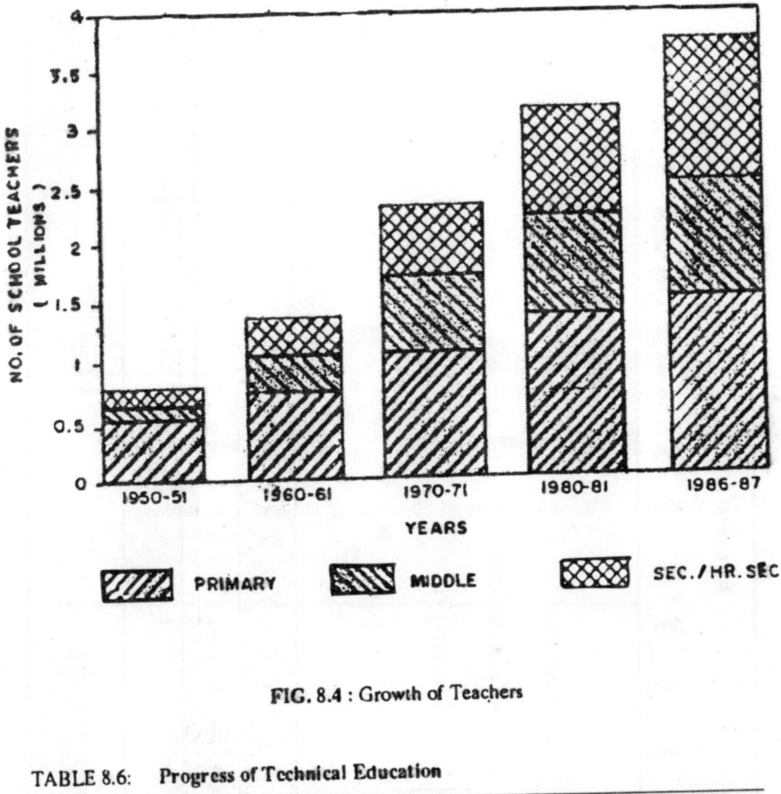

FIG. 8.4 : Growth of Teachers

TABLE 8.6: **Progress of Technical Education**

	1950-51	*1960-61*	*1970-71*	*1980-81*	*1986-87*
(1) Engineering & Technological Colleges (Degree & above level) Number of Institutions	33	78	107	120	225
Enrolment (000's)	17	48	93	130	182
(2) Engineering & Technological Colleges (Below degree level) Number of Institutions	78	130	631	885	1075*
Enrolment (000's)	36	84	133	331	303

* Relates to 1983-84.

Source: Annual Report, 1988-89, Ministry of Human Resource Development, Department of Education, Government of India.

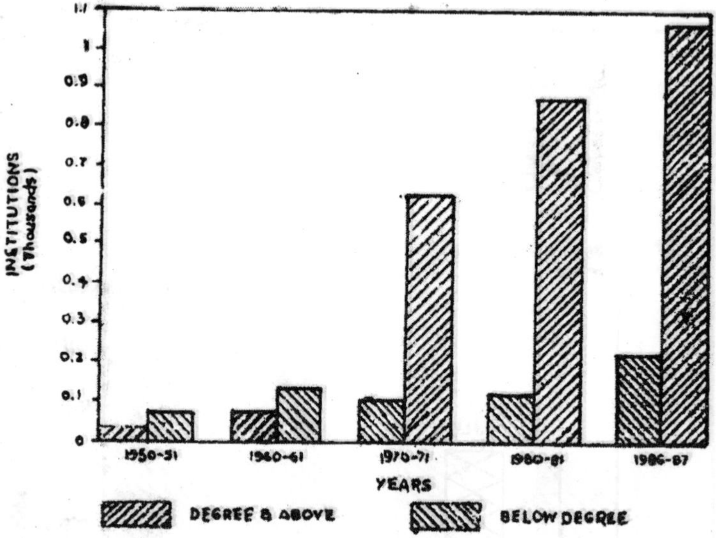

FIG. 8.5 : Technical Education (Number of Institutions)

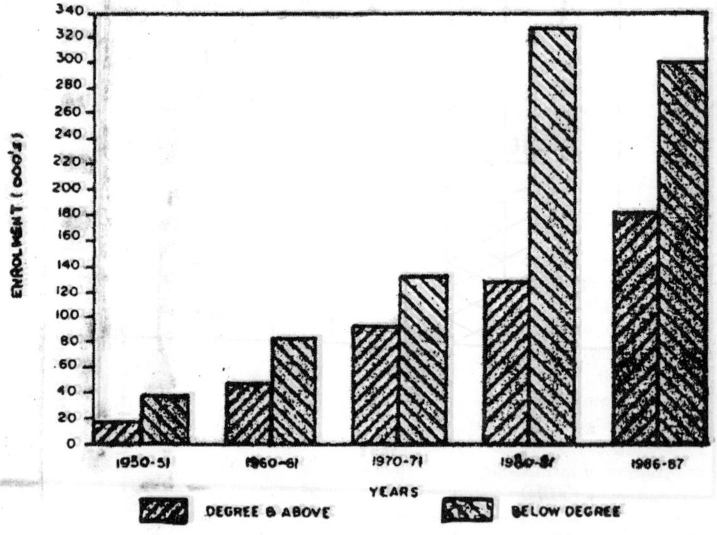

FIG. 8.6 : Technical Education (Enrolment)

Index

Aided institutions, 19
All India education profile, 103-10
Andaman & Nicobar Islands, population and institutions, 91
Andhra Pradesh, population and institutions, 67
Arunachal Pradesh, population and institutions, 92
Assam, institutions and population, 68

Bihar, population and institutions, types of, 69
Block Education Officer (BEO), 17
Budget provisions, 17

Central Advisory Board of Education (CABE), 16, 18
Central level, education administration, 15, 16
Chandigarh, population and institutions, 93

Daman and Nagar Haveli, population and institutions, 94
Decentralisation, 17
Delhi, population and institutions, 95
District Education Officer (DEO), 17
Diverse issues in education, 49-60

Education administration, 15-16; budget provision, 17; department, sectorwise, 113; National policy of, 17; planning and financing of, 17-18
Education Commission, 19
Education plans and programmes, implementation of, 15
Education stage, number of students, 114
Educational institutions, growth of, 113; programmes, implementation of, 16
Educational planning, 16
Eighth Five Year Plan, 20
Elementary education, 108; universalisation of, 19
Enrolment ratios, 21-33

Finance commission, 17
Funds, 19

Goa, Daman and Diu, population and institutions, types of, 96
Gross enrolment ratios, 21-33
Gujarat, population and institutions of, 70

Habitation, 38, 47
Haryana, population and institutions, 71
Higher Secondary, enrolment of, 100
Himachal Pradesh, population and institutions, 72

Implementation, 15-16
India, category of institutions, 105; development of education, 111-118; enrolment by classes, 104; literacy rates, 107
Indian Education Service, 18
Institutions, favourable situation, 27

Jammu & Kashmir, population and institutions of, 73

Karnataka, institutions and population of, 74
Kerala, population and institutions, types of, 75

Lakshadweep, population and institutions

of, 97
Liquidation illiteracy, 19
Lowest enrolment ratios, 25

Madhya Pradesh, population and institution, types of, 76
Maharashtra, population and institution, types of, 77
Manipur, population and institution, types of, 78
Meghalaya, institutions and population, 79
Minimum enrolment ratios, 24
Ministry of Human Resource Development (MHRD), 15
Mizoram, population and institutions, types of, 98
Municipal Corporation, 16

Nagaland institutions, 80
National Education Policy, 19-20

Orissa, population and institutions, types of, 81

Panchayat Samities, 16
Planning Commission, 16
Policy implementation, 20
Pondicherry, population and institution, types of, 99
Primary schools/sections, 38
Pupil Teacher ratios, 52, 53

Rajasthan, population and institutions, 83
Resources, 19-20

School complexes, development system, 19
Science and technology, 20
Secondary Teacher Training Institutions, 56-60
Sikkim, population and institutions, types of, 84
Stages, girls enrolment by, 115
State Advisory Board of Education, 18
State education profile, 65-88
State level, education administration, 16
States, comparative educational data, 21-34, 35, 48; trained teachers, percentage of, 55
States/Union territories, literacy rates of, 64
Statewise, per capita budgeted expenditure, 61-62

Tamil Nadu, population and institutions, types of, 85
Teachers Training Colleges, 46
Technical education, progress of, 20, 117-18
Tripura, population and institutions, types of, 86

Union Territory administration, 15
Union Territory education profile, 89-102
University Grants Commission, 16
Uttar Pradesh, population and institutions, 87

Vocational courses, 51; facilities, 27-32; education, 20
Voluntary Agencies, 19

West Bengal, population and institutions, types of, 88
Women Higher education, 109